EAGLE CLAW®

FISH COOKBOOK

How to catch, clean, store and prepare fish for good eating.
by Ken Anderson

Dorison House Publishers, Inc. Boston

As a leader in the manufacturing of quality fishing tackle for over 50 years, the Wright & McGill Co., manufacturers of world famous Eagle Claw Fishing Tackle, have been providing the American public with their products, and enhancing the enjoyment of their favorite sport, "recreational fishing."

Now, with the help of the noted outdoor author, Ken Anderson, this book will provide complete information about catching, caring, and cooking of both salt water and fresh water fish. For good fishing and good eating, it's a pleasure to present the Eagle Claw Fish Cookbook.

Ken Anderson is the author and editor of innumerable articles and books on the subject of food, cooking, sports and outdoor living. He has been Special Projects Editor for *Field and Stream,* and is currently the Executive Director of the Coffee Information Institute, and Consulting Medical Editor, J. G. Ferguson Publishing Co. His most recent book, *Sterno's Guide to the Outdoors,* published by Dorison House Publishers , is a must for campers.

Copyright © 1977 by Dorison House Publishers, Inc.
Published by Dorison House Publishers, Inc.
824 Park Square Bldg., Boston, MA 02116
ISBN: 0-916752-17-8
Library of Congress Catalog Card Number: 77-89549
Manufactured in the United States of America

Book Design: Cachalot Design Group
            Marblehead, Massachusetts

illustrations: composites of 19th Century engravings
            by Robert J. Benson

Second printing

CONTENTS

FRESH WATER
FISHING BASICS

The United States Department of Interior manages some of the biggest and finest fishing holes in the world. And in order to accommodate all the people who may decide to go fishing in a federally managed lake or stream, the Department conducts periodic surveys to learn what the American public likes to do in the way of outdoor recreation. The information obtained from the surveys is important because the types of activity most people enjoy are not necessarily the kinds of sports that get the most attention in newspaper and television coverage.

Sport fishing is just such an example of an outdoor sport that gets the short end of attention in the national media although it is in fact an activity that involves approximately 25 percent of the total population. A recent Department of Interior study found there are forty million sports fishermen in the United States. And sales of fishing licenses tend to support that figure. In 1970, the number of state fishing licenses sold in the U.S. topped the thirty million figure and the number increases every year. And as evidence of the growing popularity of sport fishing, the number of Americans participating in fresh water fishing has doubled in the past twenty years.

One important reason for the constantly increasing population of people who enjoy fishing as a sport, is that angling is a pleasant, relaxing, and yet challenging experience. While landing a fair catch of fish for the dining table or freezer is rewarding in itself, the psychological rewards are equally satisfying.

Fishing is an outdoor activity that you can indulge in by yourself, or with almost any number of people. You can compete with other fishermen for the biggest fish, the biggest total yield, or the finest fish of the day. Or you can compete with your own previous best days on a lake or river. Fishing is a way to get away from people, or to spend more time with people you like. It's also a great way to meet new friends with similar interests. In fact, there's probably no other outdoor activity that offers such a wide and varied range of recreational benefits.

Fishing in the 1970s ranked as one of the most popular of all outdoor recreation activities for Americans. According to surveys by government agencies published in "Statistical Abstracts of the United States, 1976," more than 33 million people, representing approximately 24 percent of the nation's population of twelve years of age or over, participate in sports fishing. This group of anglers formed an audience greater than the average total annual attendance of about 30 million for all major league baseball games, including the playoffs and the World Series. The number of people who reported hunting at least once a year, by comparison, totaled about 14 million. And while nearly one-fourth of all Americans chose fishing as an outdoor sport, according to the federal statistics, only 10 percent preferred bicycle riding and 5 percent indulged in golf or tennis.

Fortunately, the shorelines and surface acreages of North America's lakes, ponds, reservoirs, and streams are so vast it is possible for all of the nation's anglers to cast at the same moment without getting their lines tangled. The U.S. alone has nearly forty rivers 600 miles or more in length, two dozen fresh water lakes with surface areas of more than 150 square miles, plus 88,000 miles of tidal shoreline and thousands of square miles of salt water sounds, bays, and straits. And most of the waters are open to sports fishermen.

There are literally thousands of different kinds of fish in the waters of the world, including hundreds of species and sub-species of fresh water fish in the inland waters of this continent. One of the first steps in successful fresh water fishing is to learn what species are in the waters in which you are about to fish and to familiarize yourself with their life-styles. Understanding the life-style of the fish is an important part of the game of angling, just as it is important to know the strengths, weaknesses, and habits of your opponent in any other sport. One primary rule is that the fisherman should never underestimate the ability of the fish to outmaneuver him. In his own world a fish can be very shrewd and clever.

For example, any fish that has lived in a particular stream or lake long enough to reach maturity knows more about his immediate environment than almost any angler on the shore or in a boat. He has learned what is food and what is not food and where to find it. He has a pretty good idea of what kinds of insect life may be in season. He knows how a worm or grasshopper should act when in the water and can be expected to react with suspicion at the sight of a bait that zaps backwards through the surface of the water, as when a frantic angler retrieves his lure improperly. He can tell whether a lure that looks like an injured minnow is the real thing because he probably has seen plenty of injured minnows. Even a live bait attached to an oversized lead weight probably will be scrutinized carefully and then ignored; fish are not trained to be weight lifters.

Fortunately, most people are able to outwit a fish and some species are more cooperative than others. Bullheads, catfish, and carp, for example, thrive in ponds, shallow areas of lakes, and slow currents of rivers. They live on worms, insect larvae, and other organic foods that can be found along the muddy bottoms of streams and lakes. Since they are bottom feeders and occasionally are found in waters that are considered dirty or polluted, catfish, bullheads, and carp are sometimes shunned by anglers who hook them. However, when properly cleaned and cooked, such species are as edible as any other food fish.

Many veteran anglers take catfish and bullheads with baits that are highly inovative, ranging from balls of cheese, pieces of bread, soap and chicken blood. However, they also go for a variety of artificial lures, including jigs, spinners, and wet flies. The water depths for catfish and bullheads vary with the seasons. They are found in shallow waters in the spring and fall but when summer temperatures rise, they seek cooler waters in the deep holes and channels. But wherever they choose to spend the day, they expect to find their food along the bottoms. And while they may be suckers for strange baits and lures, catfish and bullheads are clever enough to test the bait before swallowing it. Therefore, the bait should be lightly weighted, just enough to put it on the bottom. Any significant resistance or drag on the line can cause the fish to retreat. But millions of catfish and bullheads are taken by anglers every year in America. Because of their popularity in some areas, particularly along the big rivers and lakes of the midwest and south, they frequently are served as delicacies in fine restaurants.

Carp have life-styles similar to catfish and bullheads, living on larvae, worms, dead fish, and other organic foods. They also will take a wide variety of baits and lures that are played properly along the bottoms of lakes and ponds, as well as warm streams and shallows. However, carp are probably more sensitive than catfish or bullheads about baited lines and may spit out anything that is downright suspicious. The carp may spend quite a bit of time examining the bait, nibbling and sucking at it. This activity can be misleading to a novice who sees his bobber moving about. But if the bobber suddenly drops below the surface, it's a good sign that the carp has taken the bait and that is the instant the hook must be set.

One trick in fishing for carp is in matching a small hook to a strong line. Carp have an abnormally small sucker-type mouth that can grow to tremendous size for a fresh water fish, partly because carp eat almost constantly. Some carp anglers use treble hooks to increase the chances of hooking this fish. As soon as the carp realizes he is hooked, he is likely to make a run for the nearest deep hole. The line can easily become snagged on rocks or a submerged tree limb. Any angler who wants to play a tough and wily fish on light tackle can have his hands full in landing a hooked carp. Veteran anglers who take carp for food usually concentrate on getting the fish into the boat or on shore as quickly and directly as possible.

Smallmouth bass have proved to be among the most popular fresh water fish for both sport and food for several generations. Although the smallmouth species was at one time found only in the region of the eastern Great Lakes, it has been transplanted to cool streams and lakes throughout the United States and southern Canada. The fish is most often found in cool, clear water with rocks and gravel covering the bottom, a habitat similar to that preferred by trout. In fact, the smallmouth bass tends to compete with trout in some lakes and will eat small trout along with insect larvae and crayfish.

An average size smallmouth will weigh between one and two pounds at maturity; the growth rate depends upon the temperature and other environmental factors of its habitat. Three and four pounders are unusual, but not rare, and record smallmouth weights run into two-digit numbers.

Smallmouth bass in streams tend to feed along riffles, where rocks direct currents and give the fish a chance to inspect food items floating toward him. The smallmouth also will explore areas of vegetation, sandbars, and rock piles, in a search for minnows or crayfish. But the species always appears ready to attack any kind of insect that touches the surface of the water, and this may explain why the smallmouth bass is attracted by such a wide variety of natural and artificial lures. Smallmouth bass may venture into relatively shallow waters when the water temperature is in the low sixties, Fahrenheit. But they spook easily at the sights and sounds of careless anglers, so it helps to keep a low profile. And a long cast may be needed in order to get a suspicious smallmouth to go for the lure. Interest in various lures may vary with the season; bass bugs tend to be more effective in late spring while wet flies seem to be more attractive to the smallmouth during mid-summer. However, smallmouth bass will also go for dry flies, small lures that represent frogs or grasshoppers, or bucktails played near the bottom like crayfish.

While smallmouth bass will take surface lures, they also should be retrieved in a manner that imitates the real thing. The lures should be spotted into areas where the species is likely to be foraging — near rock piles, underwater vegetation, or sunken logs. But the smallmouth is not likely to travel any great distance to check out a lure, so it should land near his hunting ground. It may have to be cast and retrieved several times before the fish will be tempted to take the lure.

Once a smallmouth bass is hooked, the angler can expect a good deal of action in landing the fish. This species offers a real test of a fisherman's ability to properly present the right kind of lure in order to hook a fish, and a test of the fisherman's skill in landing the fish once it is hooked. The smallmouth will jump, run, and fight stubbornly. And the bigger the fish, the bigger the fight.

The largemouth bass, as its name suggests, has a larger mouth than the smallmouth bass; the mouth of the largemouth extends behind the eye, unlike the smallmouth's. Also, there is a clear separation between the dorsal fin sections of the largemouth bass while in the smallmouth the segments appear continuous. The largemouth bass generally is a larger fish at maturity, particularly those taken from southern waters where weights may range upward to about twenty pounds. In northern lakes, weights usually average between two and five pounds. Like the smallmouth bass, the largemouth has been stocked successfully in waters from Canada to the Mexican border and from coast to coast. While largemouth bass are found in the same cool, clear waters as smallmouth bass, the largemouth species does better in warmer ponds and lakes and in shallow, sluggish waters where the smallmouth variety will not survive long. Weeds and other underwater vegetation offer not only protection for the largemouth bass but also good foraging areas, since the smaller fish, frogs, crayfish, and insects eaten by the bass thrive in the underwater weed patches. Largemouth bass are reluctant to leave the areas of vegetation but lures can be cast into the edges and openings to attract the attention of the largemouth.

Largemouth bass fishing is most likely to be successful when water temperatures are close to seventy degrees, although the bass begin feeding actively when water temperatures are in the sixties. As the water temperature soars into the eighties, the largemouths tend to retreat into deeper, cooler areas. Thus, many anglers find their luck improves if they try for the species during the coolest hours of night or early morning, if they fish the shallows during hot summer periods; the alternative is to fish the deeper water regions. When water temperatures become too cold for their comfort, the bass tend to move to warmer shallow areas or they may simply quit feeding in cold weather. Of course, there are exceptions to all rules of fishing and largemouth bass have been taken in warm waters on hot summer days. Generally, however, the temperature sensitivity of the largemouth bass determines where it will be found, what kind of lures to use, and how to play them. The temperature effect accounts in part for the increased yields of bass during night fishing expeditions in the hot summer months.

An entire book could be written about the different kinds of live baits and artificial lures that can be used to catch largemouth bass. More than one hundred kinds of insects, amphibians, and fish have been reported to be the favored food for bass in various parts of the continent; the list ranges from honey bees and cockroaches to tadpoles and water snakes. Ordinarily, the largemouth bass is directed toward live baits by their smell and will take a dead minnow as readily as a live one. But the bass apparently is also venturesome enough to attack any small lure that mimics a living creature passing through his neighborhood. The list of artificial lures that have claimed largemouth bass is even longer than the roster of live baits. The types that are most popular include the traditionally effective bass bugs as well as the more recently developed plastic worms, frogs, mice, and eels. Weedless spoons, plugs, spinners, bucktails, flies, and combinations of artificial lures and live baits can be equally effective. Some veteran anglers swear by such combinations as pork rind used with jigs, spinners, or spoons. The ultimate solution for most bass fishermen is to carry a wide assortment of baits and lures, and hope that the local bass don't want the lure that was left behind. It is almost literally true that every lake or pond requires a slightly different lure or technique. So it's a wise angler in strange waters who watches the local fishermen to see how they do it on a particular day. In some lakes, old-fashioned jigging still seems to be the best approach; in others, a slowly retrieved spinner may be the answer. Some fishermen prefer casting bass bugs with fly rods, others cast bugs with spinning tackle or spin-casting equipment.

Bass fishing from a boat is a necessity when working a large lake where the vegetation is near the center of the water. But casting from shore can also be fruitful if there are sunken logs, rock piles, or drop offs within reach. A dilemma facing shore fishermen is that the bass are most likely to be lurking in spots that also contain the greatest risks of snagging the lure or line. To reduce the risk, the angler should always try to cast and retrieve in a pattern that is parallel to the underwater hazard rather than at right angles to it. Patience is needed in casting for bass; it may take six to ten casts into a potential bass area before any action is registered. Also, the angler should concentrate on getting the proper action in the lure. When a bug hits the surface of the water, it should lie motionless for as long as thirty seconds before it begins moving. A frequent criticism of bass fishermen is that they sometimes become so fascinated by the noise and motion of the lure being retrieved that they forget to move the lure in the manner of the living creature it is supposed to represent.

SALT WATER
FISHING BASICS

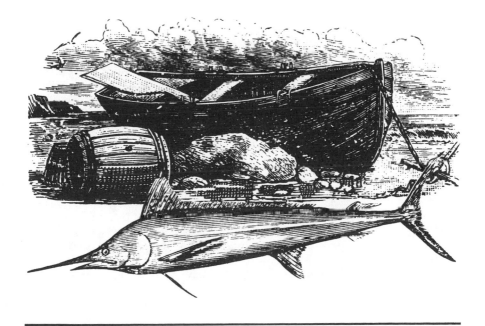

There are fish that spend part of their lives in fresh water and part in ocean water. Some live for a while in the ocean and then return to the freshwater streams of their childhood to spawn; these are called anadromous fish. There are other creatures, such as the American eel, that may live part of the time in fresh water but return to the ocean to spawn; these are referred to as catadromous species. And there are still other fish, like the milkfish, snook, and tarpon, that are identified as amphidromous, meaning they may migrate between ocean waters and fresh water rivers to feed rather than to spawn. As a result, there are a number of species of fish that can be considered either salt water or fresh water fish, or both.

The Atlantic salmon is a good size fish for fresh water angling, averaging about twelve pounds and occasionally weighing as much as fifty to one hundred pounds. It may spend up to five years in the fresh water streams of Europe and the North American continent as far south as New England. It then migrates to the ocean for as many as five additional years before returning to the fresh water streams to spawn. However, there are also landlocked varieties in lakes of New England, Canada, and elsewhere along the Atlantic coast.

The Atlantic salmon ordinarily does not feed while entering the estuaries leading to spawning streams but will for unexplained reasons take a dry fly or wet fly properly presented. It is a tough fighter and can leap several feet out of the water. Leaders generally are around ten pound test strength and ten feet in length, but even leaders of greater than ten pound test may not be strong enough. The Atlantic salmon is one of the most highly prized fish of the anadromous varieties but it's not the kind of game fish that fits into a casual weekend of fly casting into waters along the north Atlantic coasts. It takes a well planned expedition of a couple of weeks or more at the right time of the season to a likely fishing ground. However, Atlantic salmon are taken on occasion, more or less accidentally, by anglers casting for other species in the neighborhood.

The striped bass is one of the more common anadromous fishes. It is a popular game fish, a fine fish for eating, and one that is most easily accessible from heavily populated centers along both the Atlantic and Pacific coasts. Striped bass also are found in the Gulf of Mexico, and in some of the big lakes of North and South Carolina. Weights of striped bass generally range from about two to twenty pounds at maturity and record sizes of over fifty pounds have been taken.

Heavy spinning or bait casting tackle is needed to take a striped bass. Live baits and artificial lures on twenty to forty pound test lines are used in surf casting trolling, and casting from boats. Live baits may vary according to the locality and migration patterns but generally they will include squid, sand eels, mullet, clams and blood worms. Striped bass fishermen working the landlocked waters claim success with gizzard shad and plastic worms with spinners. Natural food preferences of the striped bass include shad, mullet, squid, soft clams, and sea worms. Striped bass, like the Atlantic salmon, migrate over distances of hundreds of miles. They migrate into fresh water rivers along the coasts for spawning when the temperature of the water is in the sixties, Fahrenheit; along the Atlantic Coast, spawning trips begin in mid-spring at the southern end of their range and in mid-summer in the Canadian end. The species also wander from the waters around Maryland and Virginia northward to New England and Canada during the summer, returning to southern areas again for the winter. On the Pacific Coast, there are migrations between San Francisco Bay and inland rivers draining into the Pacific. Sport fishing for striped bass usually reaches a peak during the migratory periods of the species.

The bluefish is another of the migratory species that is highly popular among salt water fishermen, although its habitat in the Western Hemisphere is restricted to Atlantic coastal waters. Yet the bluefish, like the striped bass, can be found during the year from Florida to the Maritime Provinces of Canada. Bluefish like warm sea currents and travel north during the summer, returning to the south in mid-autumn. Young bluefish tend to run in schools close to shore while the bigger members of the species seem to be loners who forage independently in deep water well offshore.

Small blues may weigh a couple of pounds and the big members of the family range upward from twenty pounds. But even the young blues put up a terrific fight, which makes the species one of the favorites of salt water fishing. In addition, the meat of the bluefish is regarded as perhaps the most tasty of all salt water species. Bluefish also are among the most voracious of all game fish. They seldom hesitate to attack another fish, including their own kind; they have been seen chasing other fish out of the water and will inflict wounds on an angler who gets an arm close to the mouth of a blue. Even the sea gulls are reluctant to tangle with a blue on a feeding rampage. The leader recommended for bluefish is a three foot wire, although the fish may shy away from a lure attached to a wire. A successful compromise can be made by attaching a large lure to a nylon leader on the assumption that the lure will prevent the teeth from cutting the nylon. Most likely a lure taken by a blue will be damaged beyond use by the time the fish has been netted or landed. Feather lures, spoons, artificial squid, and live baits are commonly used to catch blues. A dead fish can be used as bait if it is played to make it appear to be still alive.

Chumming helps attract blues, and menhadden, finely chopped, can be quite effective. Lures should be cast ahead of a school or along the side of a group of blues; casting directly into a school can cause the blues to shy away from the lure. Blues also tend to shy away from areas where there are too many boats or too many anglers casting for them. Young blues, sometimes called snappers, are attracted by chumming too. Once located, they sometimes can be taken on trout flies or small spinners. And, unlike their older generations, the leader can be a fine nylon monofilament.

A different kind of snapper, the red snapper, is caught in Atlantic waters from the Caribbean to the Mid-Atlantic states. It's a fairly large reddish fish which may weigh thirty or more pounds, a great game fish when hooked, and an excellent source of food for fillets and chowders. The red snapper frequently travels in very deep waters but occasionally forages in shallow areas of less than twenty feet in depth. The species can be taken with a rod and reel baited with a natural bait, preferably a dead bait. When taken for eating, the head and throat should be saved for chowders, stews or soups made from strips of meat along the bottom side of the head.

A popular game fish among surfcasters, particularly along the Atlantic coast from New Jersey to Florida, is the redfish, or red drum, or channel bass — actually one species with three common names. The smaller redfish, averaging perhaps five pounds in weight, are an excellent food fish but the big members of the species are taken mainly for the sport. The big redfish weigh in at forty pounds or more, with trophy specimens topping eighty pounds. Surfcasters take the redfish on the inside of sandbars and in holes near shore where they forage for shellfish. Crabs, clams, bloodworms, and mullet are among baits used. In addition, the redfish may take spoons and metal squid. Leaders of wire or heavy nylon monofilament are used. Trollers take redfish with plugs and flies, casting into the breakers along the shoreline. Cut or live bait, crabs, clams, and shrimp are effective in still fishing. The redfish takes the bait or lure carefully, then rushes toward the bottom and puts up a good fight. Young redfish, also called puppy drum, are taken on spinning tackle, using plugs and flies. Like the bigger members of the species, the young redfish approach the lure casually but make a hard fighting run when hooked. The small redfish is favored as a delicacy that is filleted and fried in deep fat but the quality of redfish meat diminishes as the fish grows larger.

Atlantic cod, which attracted Europeans to North American shores for many generations before the Pilgrims set foot on Cape Cod, is still highly regarded as a game fish by anglers of the northeastern states. From the New York City area to New England shores, some sport fishing for cod goes on the year around; the fish also is taken from North Carolina to Greenland at various times of the year. A variety of methods is used, including drift fishing, still fishing, and surf casting, although the cod generally is a deep water fish. During the summer months, cod move into waters that may be over 1,000 feet deep, returning to shallow waters close to shore during cold weather.

Small, young cod average from three to ten pounds but cod weighing thirty, forty, or fifty pounds are not unusual catches for anglers working deep waters from boats. Salt water tackle is needed with nylon monofilament line of thirty to forty pound test on a wide reel and snelled hooks of from 5/0 to 9/0 size. Eight to twelve ounce sinkers are used to hold the bait on the bottom. Baits frequently used include clams, squid, small fish, and strips of mackerel or other fish. Artificial lures such as jigs and metal squid also have proved effective. When clams are available, shells and pieces of clam meat are dropped into the water as chum.

Cod generally are shy in approaching a bait and may examine or nibble it for a short while before actually swallowing it. The angler may feel some nibble activity on the line, then nothing. The ending of nibble activity does not necessarily mean that a cod has either swiped the bait or lost interest. He may still be studying the bait and return within a few minutes to swallow the whole thing. Another enigma of cod fishing is that a cod may swallow the bait and hook without putting up a fight; sometimes the fish will stay at the spot where it took the bait. The fisherman won't feel any significant pull on the line because the many yards of monofilament attached to a heavy sinker will absorb any minor tugging on the part of the cod. At other times, a cod can be as full of fight as any other species in taking a bait.

Sometimes the bait set for cod will be taken by a smaller cousin, the haddock. Most of the haddock taken from Atlantic Ocean waters, between the Canadian Maritime Provinces and North Carolina, weigh about two or three pounds; the largest members of the haddock species weigh from fifteen to thirty or more pounds. Haddock can be distinguished from small cod fish by a black lateral line that runs along the side of the haddock from the gills to the tail. Like the cod, it rates high as a source of food for humans.

Pacific coast fishermen do take a serious interest in the Pacific halibut, which actually is a King Kong-size variation of the flounder. The Pacific halibut habitat extends from California to Alaska. Although the halibut population was virtually depleted during the 1930s, careful fish management by the Department of Interior has restored the popular game fish to numbers that permit abundant game fishing again. The halibut can be a tremendous fish. A fifty pound halibut is considered a baby while a seven foot, 200 pound specimen is too small to qualify for the record books. The halibut stays close to shore as a youngster. But as it grows older it moves into deeper waters and begins migrating over distances of hundreds of miles, feeding on worms, squid, small fish, and shellfish along the route.

The Atlantic halibut is similar to the Pacific species. But the largest Atlantic halibut ever taken were in the 600 to 700 pound category, compared to the approximately 500 pound record for Pacific halibut. Partly because of their size, both Atlantic and Pacific halibuts offer the angler a fight to remember. Most game fishing for halibut is done by drift fishing or still fishing techniques, using a very long line. The giant halibut seldom enters waters more shallow than several hundred feet in depth. Natural baits and short wire leaders are employed to get the bottom feeders.

There are three varieties of small mackerel that are of interest as game fish: Atlantic mackerel, Pacific mackerel, and tinker, or chub, mackerel. Average weights for these small mackerel are around two pounds and the biggest of their species run around six or seven pounds. They normally feed on worms, squid, shellfish, and small fish. While salt water anglers don't always try to catch the small mackerel, the mackerel frequently are attracted by baits set for other kinds of fish. The small varieties of mackerel also are taken on a variety of artificials. For anglers who want to try for Atlantic or Pacific mackerel, small spoons, flies, and jigs are recommended. And the brighter and shinier the lure the better the chances of success. Light tackle, including spinning gear, sometimes is used to take the species from bridges and piers when schools of the fish are feeding in shallow shoreline waters. Although the little mackerels are lightweight by salt water fishing standards, they can give an accounting of themselves when hooked.

Among the heavyweights of the salt water species are the marlins, sword-fish, and tunas. Blue marlins taken from Pacific waters may weigh more than 1,000 pounds while Atlantic blue marlins of more than 800 pounds have been recorded. White marlin are better fighters on a pound for pound basis but seldom grow to a size of more than 100 pounds.

Blue marlins are taken from Atlantic coastal waters as far north as New England but this species favors warm waters, so the chances of taking one are much better when fishing between the Carolinas and Florida. Charter boats with outriggers offer the best base of operations for blue marlin fishing. Small fish are used as bait and heavy 100 pound test tackle is needed. The trick needed in attracting a marlin is an ability to skip the bait. The marlin puts up a terrific fight and will run off hundreds of feet of line when hooked. He will leap nearly twenty feet above the surface, tailwalk, or make deep plunges. Because of his size and strength, the blue marlin is likely to win the struggle and break away. If the marlin doesn't escape, the angler may face an all-day hassle before bringing the trophy into the boat.

The smaller white marlin migrates as far north as Cape Cod, but like its blue marlin relatives it prefers warmer waters. Sailfishing tackle, rated at about twenty-five pounds test, is needed for white marlin fishing. Small whole fish or strip baits are favored by the species, but it also has been known to take feathers, spoons, and other artificial lures. It hits the bait with spectacular force and goes through most of the same fighting antics as the blue marlin.

Marlins tend to be loners; they travel singly or in pairs. But they seldom are found in groups. They may skip along the surface of the ocean while feeding. When the marlin breaks its skipping pattern and disappears momentarily it is a good sign that it is about to strike the bait. Some anglers set the hook as soon as the strike is felt. Others prefer to let the fish run for a few hundred feet, building momentum so the hook will become well embedded in the marlin's lip as it is set. There is a wide difference of opinion about the quality of marlin flesh as food for humans. Blue marlin meat is regarded as fair, on a scale from poor to excellent, and often is prepared as a smoked fish. White marlin meat is rated as poor.

Among the various tunas, the bluefin is probably the most popular of the big game fish of the family in both Atlantic and Pacific waters. The species grows quickly, compared to other salt-water species, reaching a size of nearly five feet and 100 pounds within five years after hatching; at ten years of age it averages close to seven feet in length and weighs more than 350 pounds. Beyond that, a bluefin tuna may reach a maximum weight of a ton or more, although the largest hook-and-line catches are in the neighborhood of 1,000 pounds. They tend to travel in schools, moving great distances in the migrations and spending much of their lives in very deep water. Bluefins tagged in the Bahamas have been caught in European waters from Norway to Spain.

Special tackle, equipped with a 130 pound test Dacron line and a long wire leader, is used for bluefin tuna fishing. In trolling, live baits such as squid or mullet are used and the bait is positioned several hundred feet behind the boat. Still fishing or drift fishing is done with live baits while chum is dropped into the water. The bait is positioned on the bottom, or well below the surface; some anglers use more than one line with baits at different levels. The hook is set quickly if the tuna takes the bait. Then follows a battle that can last for hours, especially if the tuna is a big one, as the fish dives hundreds of feet into the deepest water it can find. But if the angler has the strength and stamina to handle the tuna, he usually is well rewarded by the catch.

16

CARE OF
THE CATCH

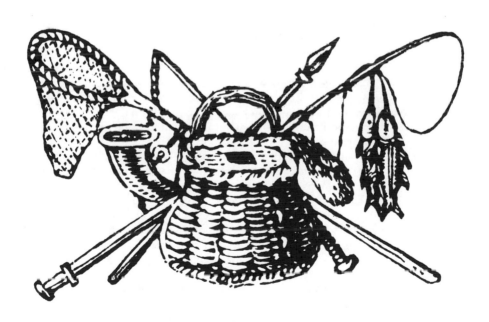

Many potentially fine fish dinners are ruined every year because anglers fail to take proper care of their catch. And like sweet corn from the garden or roasted coffee from a newly opened container, the flavor is affected by exposure to the environment — and the warmer the temperature and the longer the time of exposure the more noticeable is the loss of the flavor of freshness. Some fishermen simply toss their catch into the bottom of a boat or onto the shore, forgetting about the fish already landed while they concentrate on the next strike. But fish allowed to die in the warm sunlight deteriorate rapidly. So do fish that are allowed to drown while dangling on a stringer or while towed behind a boat. The fish may have been taken from deep cool waters but the top foot or so of the water on many lakes and ponds in North America can rise about eighty degrees Fahrenheit on a warm summer day. Once the creature is dead, chemical changes occur in the fats and proteins of the fish flesh, altering the flavor of the catch. Only cold temperatures will retard the spoilage. And once deterioration of the fish flesh begins, no cooking technique or sauce will restore the flavor of freshness.

Only in very cold weather is it safe to allow a fish to die in a boat bottom or on shore. And even then it is not recommended because of grease and grime that tend to accumulate on the surface of the fish. If a stringer is used, the fish should be held in a bucket of cold water. And the stringer should be a type that will allow the fish to remain alive in the cold water. When it is cold enough to freeze water, as in ice fishing, it is relatively safe to expose the catch to the environment. However, the catch still should be protected against the effects of cold winds that can dry out the fish flesh.

Perhaps the safest approach is to keep handy a portable ice chest that is about one-fourth filled with ice cubes or crushed ice. Most live fish placed in an ice chest will remain alive until the angler returns home or to the campsite, where the catch can be cleaned. If the angler does not have an ice chest among his gear, a bag of ice from a supermarket or tackle shop can be used to store the catch. The advantage of an ice chest is that a petcock near the bottom can be opened to allow water from the melted ice to run out. Even if the fish in the ice chest is not alive, it should not be gutted because melted water from the ice can enter the body cavity and affect the flavor of the fish.

If ice is not available, a short-range alternative is to cover the catch with a wet cloth. As water evaporates from the cloth, the fish will remain comparatively cool. And, of course, the fish should be placed in a shaded area. Some fishermen place their catches in a burlap bag in the surrounding waters but some species, especially salt water types with sharp teeth, frequently prove they are able to burrow their way out of a cloth bag and escape, along with any less adventurous species that may have been part of the catch. It might be noted, also, with regard to the use of stringers, that some species such as snappers have been known to chew through stringers and get away.

Fish that have died should be gutted, or have their entrails removed, if they are going to be kept without ice protection for any great length of time. Some anglers recommend removing the fins along with the entrails; some also remove the head and tail to save storage space. However, skinning or scaling a fish should be delayed until the catch has been delivered to the kitchen or camp because the outer layer helps prevent loss of moisture from the fleshy areas.

If for some reason it is not convenient to clean and dress the fish immediately, it can be wrapped in a good grade of paper to prevent loss of moisture, and quickly frozen. At a later time, the fish can be thawed in a pan of cold water and cleaned. The thawed fish can be cleaned almost as easily as a freshly caught fish and there is a minimum loss of flavor if the catch was frozen very soon after being hooked.

In very cold weather, a freshly caught fish can be dipped in water that is allowed to freeze as a thin protective layer of ice. The trick can be used in a similar manner for temporary storing of fish in a home freezer. A frozen fish that is kept at a temperature of zero degrees Fahrenheit in a home or commercial freezer should retain a fresh fish flavor for six to nine months, according to the U.S. Department of Agriculture. Scales can be removed from a fish by scraping gently from the tail to the head with a fish scaler or by using the dull edge of a knife. Some anglers claim there is less of a scattering of fish scales if a fork is used, with the tines pointed downward, to rake the scales from the outer surface of the fish. (Fig. 1)

Some species, such as carp and buffalo fish, can be cleaned by a technique known as fleecing. A sharp knife is placed at the tail end of the fish and a cut is made under the scales and between the inner and outer layers of skin. The scales can then be peeled off in a more or less continuous sheet. The inner skin remains to help hold the flesh together during the cooking process. All fish should be washed carefully before and after removing the scales. Species taken from mud-bottom lakes and ponds may have a thin layer of slime that should be scraped off carefully after the scaling; the fish should be given an additional rinsing to make sure the slime, which can give the fish a "muddy flavor," has been removed.

Bullheads and their catfish cousins can be skinned in two ways. One way is to begin a cut behind the adipose fin, or the fleshy fin near the tail. Cut forward to the head and down to the backbone. Then bend the head forward to break the backbone. Next, insert a finger over the end of the backbone and into the rib cage. Pull the head backward and peel the skin off the flesh. The entrails will pull free with the head. The second way is to make a cut through the skin across the back at the base of the head of the fish. Then grasp the skin with a pair of pliers and pull off the skin. Next, bend down the head to break the backbone and pull off the head with the entrails. Some anglers find the skin is pulled off the catfish with less difficulty if a stiff wire or piece of line is run through the head of the fish and anchored to a nail on a post or a tree limb, so both hands can be free to pull back on the skin.

For most fish, the entrails can be removed simply by cutting open the belly from the vent to the head. If the head is to be removed, a cut should be made just behind the gills. This spot, sometimes identified as the collarbone area of the fish, is approximately where the backbone joins the head. By forcing the head of the fish over the edge of a cutting board or table after making the collarbone cut, the head bone should break away from the backbone. (Figs. 2, 3 & 4)

To remove the large back fin, also called the dorsal fin, the flesh should be cut along each side of the fin until it can be pulled out. Novice fish cleaners sometimes try to remove the dorsal fin by cutting it to the level of the back flesh with a sharp knife or kitchen shears, not realizing that the fin is "rooted" in the flesh with a set of bones that would be left behind in the meat. (Fig. 5)

After the scales, entrails, head, tail, and fins have been removed, the fish is considered pan-dressed. However, the cook or person eating the fish may prefer to prepare the specimen with only the scales or skin and entrails removed. The choice is a personal matter. If the fish is large enough to be cut into steaks, the head, fins, and tail are removed anyway. And only the flesh between the head and tail is used in making fillets.

In calculating the amount of edible flesh available for a serving, the rule of thumb is that approximately 45 percent of a whole fish can be used. When a fish has been pan-dressed, about 67 percent of the weight is edible. About 84 percent of a fish steak can be eaten, the remainder being bone. But a fish fillet is 100 percent meat.

Filleting

Filleting a fish requires a good knife and a little practice. A good filleting knife should have a thin, flexible, straight-edged blade that is very sharp. Some professional butchers make the first filleting cut at the head end of the fish, others recommend starting at the tail end and working toward the head. From either starting point, the knife should cut down to the backbone from the back of the fish. But the blade should not be allowed to cut through the backbone. After the first cut is made, turn the knife blade flat and cut the flesh along the backbone, allowing the knife to run over the rib bones. Next, separate the ribs from each fillet by running the knife under the ribs to the end, making a shallow cut along them. The fillet should be lifted free of the rest of the fish as a single piece of meat. It may be necessary to make a small extra cut to free the fillet from the tail.

After the first fillet has been removed, turn the fish over and repeat the procedure to cut the fillet from the other side. If it is desirable to remove the skin from the fillet, lay the fillet skin side down on a cutting board. Hold the tail of the fillet with the fingers and make a cut through the flesh to, but not through, the skin at a point about one-half inch from the end of the fillet. Then flatten the knife blade against the skin and slide the knife forward while holding the skin firmly between the fingers. It may help to move the knife blade in a seesaw pattern with the pressure of the knife against the skin but not pressed hard enough to cut the skin. (Figs. 7, 8 & 9)

Most fish fillets are cut as single fillets, that is one side of a fish from head to tail. However, smaller fish sometimes are cut as butterfly fillets, with both sides removed from the backbone and ribs of the fish but held together by the uncut flesh and skin of the belly. However, butterfly filleting must be planned in advance of gutting the fish so that a standard belly cut is not made to remove the entrails.

A fish fillet is ready to cook by any of the basic methods of preparation — frying, baking, boiling, broiling, or steaming in an almost infinite variety of dishes. A fillet is also an ideal form of fish preparation for freezing for later use because it offers the maximum amount of fish flesh in the minimum amount of storage space. Some experts recommend that fillets to be frozen be dipped in a 5 percent salt solution before wrapping and freezing. A 5 percent salt solution can

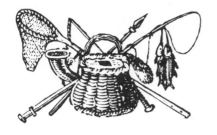

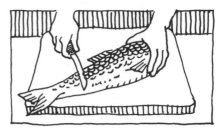

1. SCALING

2. CLEANING

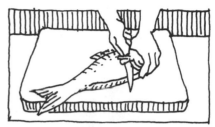

3. REMOVING HEAD

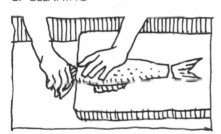

4. REMOVING HEAD · TAIL

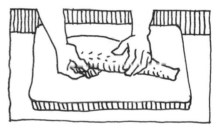

5. REMOVING FINS

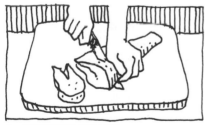

6. CUTTING STEAKS

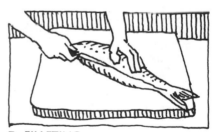

7. FILLETING

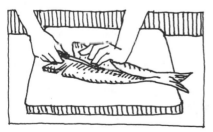

8. FILLETING

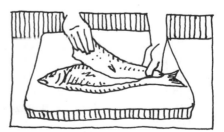

9. FILLETING

be made from two-thirds cup of salt dissolved in one gallon of water. The fillet should be held in the salt solution for about thirty seconds. Frozen fillets can be cooked without thawing if additional cooking time is allowed and if there are no plans for breading or stuffing the fillets. However, fish fillets are easier to handle for cooking if they have been allowed to thaw overnight in a refrigerator or left at room temperature for three or four hours before the start of cooking preparations.

Fish Steaks

Large pan-dressed fish can be cut into steaks. Steaks are made by cutting crosswise through the dressed fish with a sharp knife. The cuts should be made at intervals of from three-fourths of an inch to one inch to provide steaks of an equivalent thickness. A cross section of the backbone should be the only bone remaining in the fish steak after it has been cut. (Fig. 6) Steaks, like fillets, can be cooked immediately or frozen for later use. When fish steaks are to be frozen, the steaks should be given the thirty second dip in a 5 percent salt water solution made with the formula described previously for use in preparing fish fillets for freezing. Although fish steaks contain slightly less meat per pound than fish fillets, the proportions are approximately equivalent for estimating the amount needed for an average serving. About one pound of fish steaks should be enough for three servings, with a little less for small children and a little more per serving for adults.

Fish steaks and fillets can be cut into smaller boneless chunks for use in special meals such as fish kabobs. Fillets may be cut into one-inch wide strips that can be rolled and placed on skewers or chunks cut from firm-fleshed fish steaks can be placed on skewers or used in other special dishes including stews, soups, chowders, and casseroles. Small chunks of fish also are used in deep-fat frying recipes, such as Japanese-style tempura.

Raw Fish

Before the days of refrigeration, people devised methods of fish preparation for future use that included salting, smoking, pickling, drying, etc. They also found ways of treating raw fish with citrus juices, ginger, or other food items which made the fish pleasantly edible without further preparation. The technique of preparing raw fish, called ceviche in Latin America and sashimi in Japan, cannot be used for any or all types of fish with equal results. It is not recommended for freshwater species, particularly not northern pike or lake trout, because freshwater fish are vulnerable to infestation by tapeworms and other organisms that can be passed along to humans who eat the raw fish flesh. Thus, freshwater fish should always be well cooked before eating. But saltwater fish rarely if ever harbor infectious organisms that can be transmitted to humans through eating and many of the popular sea species can be used in raw fish dishes. The species include sole, flounder, seabass, tuna, and similar fish. The skin and any dark portion of the flesh are removed and the white meat is cut into small, thin slices and chilled in a marinade of the juice of limes and/or lemons, chopped onions, and spices. It may be kept for several days before eating. The Japanese dip the raw fish pieces in a mixture of soy sauce and ginger or dry mustard dissolved in hot water. The Japanese, who consume about ten times as much fish per person as Americans, regard the raw fish sashimi as the most delightful of culinary delicacies.

Ordinarily, there is no "fishy" odor to fresh raw fish. The odor of a freshly caught fish is hardly noticeable. The so-called "fishy" smell of a fish does not become disagreeably strong until some time after it has been taken from the water. The flesh of a fish just taken from the water should be firm and not separated from the bones. One traditional test is to push a finger into the flesh of a fish, if the indentation remains the fish has been out of the water too long. If the fish is fresh, the indentation made by the finger should quickly disappear, just as it should when you poke a finger into your own living flesh.

Three other tests of the quality of your catch involve the skin, eyes, and gills. A good fresh fish should have shiny skin, with unfaded color. When first taken from the water, most fish have an irridescent appearance. Each species has characteristic markings and colors which tend to fade and become more difficult to distinguish when the fish has been out of the water too long. The eyes of a fresh fish should be bright, clear, and full. When a fish has lost the bright transparency in its eyes and the eyes have become cloudy or pinkish in color, it has begun to deteriorate. Also, the eyes of a freshly caught fish may tend to protrude, but after it has been out of the water for a while, the eyes develop a sunken appearance. The gills of a freshly caught fish should be red and free of slime. After it has been exposed to the air for a while, the gills gradually change in color from red to pink and later to gray, brown, or a greenish shade.

Generally, a catch that is quickly and properly prepared for freezing will maintain most of the characteristics of freshly caught fish. Frozen fish should have little or no odor and no browning or drying around the edges. Virtually all deterioration is prevented when fish are properly held at temperatures of zero degrees Fahrenheit or below while wrapped in moisture proof material with little or no air space between the fish and the wrapper. However, even properly packaged and frozen fish should not be refrozen once it has been allowed to thaw, for it will not regain its fresh quality when refrozen after thawing.

PRESERVING
THE CATCH

Freezing Fish

There is little doubt that a fresh fish tastes better than one that has been frozen. But when a large catch needs to be protected against deterioration, freezing probably is the best method. The first step, of course, is to clean and dress the fish according to the way it will be cooked — as fillets, steaks, or dressed with or without the head and tail. It is not recommended that a fish be frozen before it is properly cleaned. And the fish should be cleaned and frozen the same day it is caught, if at all possible.

In order to freeze fish quickly and thoroughly, the freezer temperature should be adjusted to a level of ten degrees Fahrenheit, or less. And freezer trays should not be overcrowded with fresh fish to be frozen. The recommended maximum storage period for lean fish such as bass, cod, perch, pike, sunfish, etc., is six to eight months. For fatty fish, including catfish, herring, mackerel, and salmon, the time limit is shorter, or between two and four months.

All anglers do not agree on the question of whether or not the fish should be dipped in a brine or antioxidant before freezing. Commercial fish freezers believe it is better to use brine and/or an antioxidant, particularly with cut-up pieces of fish. The practice is accepted by the Food and Drug Administration in its regulations for preserving fish.

Fatty fish and lean fish require different kinds of treatment.

For lean fish: immerse the fish in a brine solution for thirty seconds. The brine is prepared by dissolving two-thirds of a cup of salt in one gallon of water.

For fatty fish: Immerse for twenty seconds in a solution of ascorbic acid. The ascorbic acid solution is prepared by dissolving two teaspoonsful of ascorbic acid in one quart of water.

Improper or poorly done packaging is the cause for much of the loss of quality in frozen fish. The fish must be well protected by wrapping it tightly in moisture-proof and vapor-proof packaging material. Tight wrapping helps remove as much air as possible.

Equipment needed:
Moisture-vapor-proof wrapping, such as:
    Freezer paper
    Aluminum foil (heavy duty)
    Plastic wrap (heavy duty)
    Plastic bags (heavy duty) with ties
Rigid containers with lids, such as:
    Plastic freezer containers
    Milk cartons
    Large cans, including coffee cans, shortening containers
    Freezer tape
    Labels and marking pens

Freeze the fish into meal-size units for ease in thawing. (A good rule of thumb for estimating meal-size units is to figure about five ounces of fish fillet, or one-third of a pound, per person. Thus, one pound of fillets would be a meal-size unit for three persons, two pounds for six persons, etc.) Label each package with the kind of fish, the weight or number of servings per package, and the date.

Packaging Fillets or Steaks:

After immersing in salt or ascorbic acid solution, drain the fish pieces thoroughly. To make separation easier when thawing, put several sheets of freezer paper between the pieces. Then overwrap snugly with moisture-vapor-proof packaging material. Seal with freezer tape, label, and freeze.

Packaging Whole Fish:

Whole fish usually are not dipped in brine or ascorbic acid before freezing. Care must be taken when packaging to avoid punctures in the wrapping materials from bones or other sharp edges of the fish portions.

1. Wrap carefully in moisture-vapor-proof material, seal, and for extra protection, overwrap and seal in a plastic bag. If desired, a piece of freezer paper placed in the body cavity will keep the sides separated for easier thawing. Label the package and freeze.
2. When using a rigid freezer container, place the fish in the container, surrounded by crushed ice. Pour in water, making sure the fish is completely covered, and freeze. When solid, a plastic lid or aluminum foil can be fastened on with freezer tape. Be sure to label the package.
3. Ice glazing fish, while not easy to do, is a very satisfactory method of freezing whole fish when the process is done properly. When preparing fish for ice-glazing, eviscerate it but do not remove the skin from the fish. Place the unwrapped fish in the freezer and allow it to freeze hard. Meanwhile, chill shallow trays and a container of water in the freezer. Next, dip the frozen fish in the ice water and place it in one of the chilled trays. Then freeze the fish in the ice water, repeating the procedure if necessary until a layer of ice-glaze has built up to a thickness of about one-eighth of an inch. Wrap the ice-glazed fish in moisture-vapor-proof material to protect the ice seal. Seal the covering tightly with freezer tape and label the package.

Frozen fish can be cooked without first thawing it, but it must be cooked longer. For best results when thawing, defrost the unopened package slowly in the refrigerator. This reduces the loss of flavorful fish juices. Thawing in the refrigerator takes about five hours per pound of fish. Once the fish is thawed, cook it as soon as possible.

Smoking Fish

There are two basic methods of preserving fish by smoking: hot smoking and cold smoking. Hot smoking is essentially a cooking process. Fish prepared in this manner should be eaten within a few days or frozen for storage. Cold smoking is a technique used to preserve fish for a longer period of time. When cured by cold smoking, the fish can be packaged and placed in cold storage (thirty-two to forty degrees Fahrenheit) for up to three months. However, cold smoked fish must be cooked before eating. The cold smoking process is accomplished in a specially constructed smoke chamber at a temperature of about seventy degrees Fahrenheit, but not exceeding ninety degrees Fahrenheit. There are many types of smokers that can be built for home or camp use, from simple to elaborate in design and structure. The important requirement is the careful control of heat and air circulation. Many anglers find it easier to buy an inexpensive commercially built smoker, either a portable outdoor type or a permanent one, than to make an investment of time and materials in building a fish smoker. One popular commercial model that costs less than forty dollars runs on alternating electric current and handles up to eighteen pounds of fish at a time.

When necessary to avoid wasting a good catch of fish, workable smoking chambers can be constructed from a variety of objects found around home or camp, such as cardboard boxes, tin cans, tarpaulins, etc. The main objective is to catch the smoke and avoid excessive heat on the fish. For hot smoking, even a backyard barbecue grill with a cover can be used. When on a fishing or camping trip, a do-it-yourself device may be the only way if a permanent smoker is not available. Any dry non-resinous wood can be used for the fire. Nut or fruit woods are favored for their rich smoky taste. It may be easier to work with hardwood chips or sawdust because they smoulder slowly, thereby giving off more of the desired smoke. The type of wood gives a distinctive flavor and hickory wood, when available, is a popular, reliable species recommended for beginners. After a bit of experience, the angler may decide to experiment with the wood of one of the fruit trees. In the Florida area, fish smokers make use of coconut husks, mangrove and cypress woods, and palmetto roots. Woods that should be avoided because of their resin are green woods and pine.

How the fish is dressed for smoking depends upon the size, the kind of fish and the method to be used. Fillets, chunks, or whole fish can be smoked. Anglers frequently split the fish open by cutting along the backbone but without cutting through the belly skin. This kind of cut allows the fish to lie flat on the smokehouse tray. If racks are used in the smoker rather than trays, the fish head can be left on to make racking easier.

It is necessary to scrape the body cavity of the fish very clean, removing all traces of viscera, blood, and membranes. In general, fish are then leached of any remaining blood by smoking the flesh in a brine bath for thirty minutes. The brine is prepared by dissolving one cup of salt in one gallon of water. At this point, three things will determine the length of time the fish can be preserved by smoking: the salting, or brining; the smoking period, and the temperature.

Cold Smoking — Dry Salt Method

After the initial brine leaching, rinse the fish in fresh water and drain it thoroughly to remove all excess moisture. Then dredge the fish in a container of fine-grained salt. Whatever salt sticks to the fish should be allowed to remain. Have a shallow wooden box ready. It must be a container from which moisture can drain. Place the fish in single layers on a one-half inch thick layer of pickling salt in the wooden box. Between each layer of fish scatter a layer of salt. Then, remove the salt in six hours if the fish have been split; the salt should remain for twelve hours if the fish are whole.

Rinse the fish in fresh water and set them outside to air-dry in the shade for three hours or until a shiny casing, called a pellicle, forms. The drying process must not be done in sunlight because the sun rays can results in an uneven rusted appearance. Air drying can be done on the trays of racks of the smokehouse. They can be placed skin side down and uncrowded as when they are smoked, or they can be air-dried in special drying racks, as long as the fish can later be transferred to the smokehouse without damaging the pellicle.

When the initial fire is burning well in the smokehouse, however it is made, with hardwood, charcoal briquettes, or electric plate, fine hardwood chips or sawdust should be added to produce a dense smouldering smoke with little heat. Ideally, the temperature of the smoke should be about seventy degrees Fahrenheit. The smoking period can be light, lasting about twenty-four hours, to preserve the fish for about two weeks while refrigerated. The longer the curing time in the smoke, the longer the fish can be stored. Fish smoked for a period of four or five days should keep for several months.

In order to determine if the fish is smoked as you prefer it, set aside one of the fish for testing occasionally. When ready, air dry the fish again in a cool place. The fish can then be packaged in plastic wrap and stored at a temperature of thirty-two to forty degrees Fahrenheit.

Hot Smoking — Brine Method

After the fish have been leached of blood in the first brine solution, they are given a second brine bath. The formula for the second brine solution varies according to individual taste. Some anglers like a simple salt solution. Others add sugar and spices to the brine. A good proportion of ingredients is one cup of salt and one-half cup of brown sugar to one gallon of water. Two or three teaspoons of crushed black pepper and several tablespoons of crushed bay leaves can be added, if desired.

Soak the fish in this brine for three or four hours or longer, according to their size. Remove the brine, drain, and pat dry with paper towels, or air dry them. Place the fish on smokehouse trays, skin side down. During the first stage of smoking, keep the smoke temperature relatively low, around 100 degrees Fahrenheit and no more than 120 degrees Fahrenheit. How long the fish are cured in the smoke is determined in part by the smoke flavor wanted. Generally, the time period is three to four hours.

Next, raise the temperature to 165 to 180 degrees Fahrenheit for about one hour. This finishes the smoking process by cooking the fish. As in cold smoking, it is a good idea to remove a piece of fish occasionally and test it for the proper stage of doneness. The fish should be ready to eat after the final stage of hot smoking. But if it is to be stored, cool it and it can be stored in a refrigerator for several weeks. Hot smoked fish also can be packaged and frozen in the same way that fresh fish are frozen for storage.

Pickling Fish

There is no general procedure for preserving fish by pickling. Generally, the ingredients include vinegar, salt, and spices. Following are several suggested recipes for preparing pickled fish:

Fill a one quart container with bite-size chunks of a fresh-water fish, such as pike. Then add:

Three tablespoons of salt
Four tablespoons of sugar
Two teaspoons of pickling spice
One onion, chopped

Then fill the remaining space in the container with vinegar. Place the container in a refrigerator and let it stand for about four days before serving.

Ceviche, or Seviche

For lean, white fleshed saltwater fish:

Prepare a marinade of the juice of three or four fresh lemons and three or four fresh limes, plus:

One cup of salad oil
One large onion, finely chopped
Two garlic cloves, minced
Two teaspoons coriander seeds, crushed
Two green chili peppers
Three or four bay leaves

Cut one pound of flounder, sea bass, or similar saltwater fish into bite-size pieces and place them in the bottom of a bowl. Pour the marinade over the fish chunks and set the bowl in a refrigerator. Let the mixture remain in the refrigerator for one or two days, stirring the mixture occasionally so that all surfaces of the fish pieces can be exposed to marinade. Serve cold.

For fatty saltwater fish:

Prepare a layer of fresh vegetables, including chopped onion, chopped carrots, and chopped parsley, mixed with cloves, peppercorns, and bay leaves, on the bottom of a large skillet. Remove the heads and tails of several mackerel or similar fatty fish. Wash the fish carefully, dry with paper towels, and cover with a light coating of salt. Place the salted fish on top of the layer of vegetables and spices.

Prepare a mixture of dry white wine and white vinegar, half and half, in an amount enough to cover the fish and vegetables. Pour the mixture over the fish and vegetable-spice mixture and bring the fluid to a boil. Then reduce the heat and let the contents of the skillet simmer for five to ten minutes. Let the skillet contents cool.

Remove the fish to a large bowl and pour the liquid from the skillet over the fish, using a sieve. Some of the vegetable-spice mixture can be squeezed through the sieve with the fluid by pressing the softened foods with a spoon. Add salad oil to the fluid and place the bowl of fish and marinade in a refrigerator to keep the food cold until it is served.

For pickled herring:
One pound of pan-dressed herring
One ounce allspice
Two bay leaves
Four ounces sugar
A half-dozen peppercorns
One onion, finely chopped
One cup vinegar

Soak the herring overnight. Skin and fillet the fish. Then cut the fillets into bite-size pieces and place in the bottom of a bowl. Mix the vinegar with the other ingredients and pour over the fish. Place the bowl containing the fish and marinade in a refrigerator for several hours before serving.

For pickled fried fish:

Prepare a marinade of the following ingredients:
Three cups vinegar
Two bay leaves
Two onions, chopped
One teaspoon peppercorns

Place the ingredients in a saucepan and cook until the onions are soft. Prepare a sauce of one ounce of curry powder, one tablespoon of vinegar, and flour to thicken. Cut two pounds of fish fillets into chunks about one and a half inches thick. Dip in a mixture of flour, salt, and pepper, to taste, and fry in hot fat until done. Place the cooked fish in a deep dish. Add the sauce to the marinade and pour the mixture over the fish. Place in a refrigerator for two days and serve cold.

Drying Fish

Fish drying is one preservation technique that requires conditions not likely to be found in areas where fish are abundant. The method requires clean dry air, low humidity, and a fairly constant breeze. However, it is one of the oldest known methods of preserving fish and is still used in many parts of the world. The best known method of drying fish is called dry salting. Certain species of saltwater fish, such as cod, herring, and mackerel, are often salted and dried as a means of preservation. Almost any other fish can be preserved this way, however. Lean fish, of course, have a longer storage life than fatty fish. To prepare fish for drying, cut open the throat, remove the gills and bleed them as soon as they have been landed. Remove the head, but leave the collarplate below the gills. Cut the fish open so they will lie flat, either cutting through the backbone or the belly. And clean them thoroughly, inside and out.

Meanwhile, prepare a bleaching brine by dissolving one cup of salt in one gallon of water. Soak the fish in the brine for thirty minutes. Then drain well until all the obvious moisture is gone. Next, dredge the fish in a container of pickling salt. Use about one pound of salt to four pounds of fish. All the fish are to accumulate as much of the salt as possible, inside and out. Then place the fish on drying racks in a shady but breezy location. Good ventilation with shade is necessary to salt dry fish properly.

Insects can be kept away by propping cheesecloth over the drying racks or by burning a smoky fire near the drying area. Night moisture causes mold, so the fish need to be removed to an inside shelter at night. When the fish are inside for the night, place heavy weights on them to help press out excess moisture. If poor weather requires that you keep the fish indoors for a day or more, salt again lightly. Any loose salt should be brushed off when the fish are returned to the outside for further drying. Depending upon the size of the fish, or the weather (humidity lengthens the drying period), dry the fish for at least forty-eight hours. The whole process may take a week or longer. But it should not be rushed.

Before storing the dry-salted fish, test the flesh for dryness by pressing a thick section of the meat. If no impression can be made in the flesh, it can be considered to be dry. Dried fish should be wrapped in wax paper and packed in wooden boxes for storage in a cool, dark place. If this packaging method is not practical, dried fish can be packaged for freezing. Dry-salted fish need to be freshened for cooking by soaking them in water for up to twelve hours to restore moisture and remove excess salt.

FRYING FISH

The flesh of a freshly caught fish can be compared to a freshly laid egg of a chicken. Each is naturally tender and juicy. If an egg, or a fish, has lost its freshness, no sauces or herbs can save it. Cooking a fish also is like cooking an egg in the matter of timing. Overcooking either can result in dryness and toughness. There is nothing more important in proper fish cookery than carefully checking the time the catch is exposed to the cooking heat and watching for the quality frequently termed, for lack of a more appropriate word, "doneness." Cooking times usually are given in recipes. But it should be remembered that these times are only estimates. It is better for each person who cooks fish to learn how to recognize when a fish is properly cooked. And it is always better to err on the side of a fish dish that is slightly underdone than one that is overly cooked.

Just as the cooking process changes an egg white from a watery, translucent appearance to one that is white and opaque, it produces similar changes in fish flesh. When the fish at the center of its thickest part has changed to an opaque, whitish color, it should be done. In order to know when this important instant occurs, begin testing the flesh with a fork about halfway or less through the prescribed cooking time listed in the recipe. When cooked, the flesh will flake and pull away from the bones without difficulty.

Keep in mind that cooking is like a chemical process in which time is only one factor to consider. Others are the temperature of the heat and how it is applied to the flesh, the size of the fish, etc.

In determining how much fish to cook for a meal so that each person receives an average serving, figure one pound of whole fish per portion, or one-half pound of pan-dressed fish, one-half pound of fish steaks, or one-third to one-half pound of fish fillets. The differences are determined by the proportion of edible meat that is available in the various stages of dressing a fish. Obviously, a boneless fillet that has been skinned is about 100 percent edible meat whereas only about half of a whole fish will actually be edible.

Pan-Frying Fish Tips

1. Use a heavy skillet or frying pan for better temperature control.

2. Heat about one-eighth of an inch of fat or oil in the bottom of the skillet. If butter is used as the fat, mix in a small amount of some other fat or cooking oil, such as olive oil or salad oil. Butter by itself tends to burn quickly and may become smokey.

3. If a temperature control is used, set the temperature for about 350 degrees Fahrenheit.

4. Keep the cooking fat hot but not hot enough to become smokey.

5. Generally, the fish is dipped in a liquid which can be milk or beaten egg or both, then coated with a breading of crumbs. The layer of liquid and bread crumbs, or a similar cereal product, acts as a protective coating from the heat.

6. Don't overload the pan with fish. Do one layer at a time.

7. Fry the fish for about four or five minutes on one side, or until the bottom side has become browned. Then turn the fish gently so the flesh will not become torn, and brown the other side about four or five minutes.

8. Test the doneness of the fish with a fork. If it doesn't flake, it probably isn't quite done.

9. Bigger fish will take longer to reach the doneness stage than small fish.

10. Drain the fish on paper towels to absorb the excess cooking fat or oil and serve it while it is still hot.

For a typical recipe to serve six people, using three pounds of pan-dressed fish, you will need the following ingredients for dipping fish to be fried:

¼ cup Milk   Dash Pepper
1½ cups Dry Bread or Cracker   1 Egg, beaten
   Crumbs or Cereal, such as Cornmeal   1 teaspoon Salt

All the ingredients except the bread crumbs should be mixed thoroughly before dipping the fish. Then roll the fish in the crumbs or cereal.

The amount of fat for frying will depend upon the size of the skillet; as noted above it should be sufficient to cover the inside of the skillet to a depth of at least one-eighth of an inch. A novice at fish cookery can start with a couple of small, freshwater pan fish. A pound of dressed pan fish will be sufficient for a main dish meal for two people.

PAN-FRIED PAN FISH

2 servings

1 pound small, dressed Fish   1 tablespoon Margarine, or good
¼ cup Cornmeal   Cooking Oil
½ teaspoon Salt

Clean, wash, and drain the fish. Set aside for a few moments. Mix the cornmeal and salt thoroughly. If cornmeal is not available, use ordinary flour, or dried bread crumbs. Dip the fish in the cornmeal-salt mixture.

Heat the margarine or cooking oil in a heavy skillet. Place the fish in the heated skillet and cook it until the fish is browned on one side. This takes about 5 minutes.

Then gently turn the fish and add a little more fat or cooking oil if needed. Fry the other side for about 5 minutes, or until it is browned on the other side. Test the flesh of the fish with a fork to see if it flakes easily. If it does, the fish is ready to serve.

As noted earlier in this chapter, fresh fish frequently have a better flavor when the fish is covered with a protective coating of flour and egg or milk, or both, during the pan frying process. Here is a recipe that moves on to the next step of fish cookery:

BATTER-FRIED FISH
---

4 servings

2 pounds Fish fillets	½ teaspoon Salt
1 teaspoon Salt	¼ teaspoon Pepper
1 cup sifted Flour	¾ cup Milk
1 teaspoon Baking Powder	1 Egg, beaten
1 teaspoon Marjoram	

Remove skin and bone from fish, unless fillets have been trimmed of non-edible material. Cut the fillets into cubes about one inch per side. Sprinkle with salt. Mix together the flour, baking powder, marjoram, salt, and pepper. Combine milk and egg and blend into flour mixture.

Dip cubes of fish flesh in the batter. Place the dipped cubes in a well-greased skillet and fry until golden brown on all sides. Serve.

SCOTTISH FRIED BREAKFAST TROUT
---

2 servings

4 Trout, pan-dressed	2 ounces Bacon Fat, or other Fat
½ pint Milk	As desired Salt
1 cup coarse Oatmeal	As desired Pepper

Salt and pepper the trout the night before and refrigerate them. In the morning, dry the fish and cut them open to remove the bones. Dip the fish in the milk, then roll them in the oatmeal.

Fry the fish in hot fat four or five minutes on each side until they are browned and the flesh flakes easily. Drain on paper towels. Serve the fish hot with a little butter on the fish, sliced lemon, and poached eggs.

6 servings

6 fillets, any lean, white flesh Fish
1 Egg, beaten
¼ teaspoon Ground Chilies
1 teaspoon Ground Tumeric
1 teaspoon Salt
½ tablespoon Lemon Juice, or juice of
   ½ lemon

1 Onion, medium, chopped fine
1 Garlic Clove
4 tablespoons toasted Bread Crumbs
2 tablespoons Fat, or enough to make
   ⅛ inch layer in skillet

Combine egg, ground chilies, tumeric, salt, lemon juice, and onion. Marinate fish fillets in the mixture and refrigerate for one hour, turning occasionally. Cut garlic cloves into a few pieces and begin heating the fat (bacon fat, or a mixture of butter and olive oil) in a skillet. Sauté the garlic lightly in the fat and remove from heat.

Dip the marinated fish fillets in the toasted bread crumbs. When fat is sizzling, add the fillets and fry them until they are golden brown, or flake easily when fork tested. Serve on a hot platter with parsley and sliced lemon.

BASS CURRY

6 servings

2 pounds Bass fillets
1½ cups Apples, chopped, peeled
1 cup sliced Onions
1 Garlic Clove, minced
3 tablespoons Butter or Margarine
1 (16-Ounce) can Tomatoes, or fresh
   Tomato wedges

4 teaspoons Flour
1 teaspoon Salt
1 teaspoon Curry Powder
½ teaspoon Chili Powder
¼ teaspoon Ginger, powdered
6 cups cooked Rice

Thaw fish, if frozen. Cut fillets into one-inch chunks. Cook apples, onions, and garlic in butter or margarine in a skillet until tender. Add tomatoes and mix. Blend in flour and seasonings. Cover and simmer 20 minutes or until flavors are blended, stirring occasionally. Add fish chunks and simmer 10 minutes, or until fish flakes easily when fork tested. Serve on hot cooked rice.

6 servings

2 pounds Fish fillets
1 (20-ounce) can Pineapple chunks
1¼ cups Pineapple syrup and water
¼ cup Cider Vinegar
¼ cup Brown Sugar
3 tablespoons Cornstarch
1 tablespoon Soy Sauce
1½ teaspoons Salt
½ teaspoon Garlic Salt

3 tablespoons Cooking Oil
1 (6-ounce) can Water Chestnuts,
   drained and sliced
1 Green Pepper, cut into one-inch
   squares
1 medium Tomato, cut into thin
   wedges
6 cups hot cooked Rice

Thaw fish, if frozen. Cut fish into one-inch chunks. Drain pineapple chunks, reserve syrup and add enough water to syrup to make one and one fourth cups of liquid. Combine liquid, vinegar, brown sugar, corn starch, soy sauce, and salts, and blend well.

Cook fish in oil in a 12-inch skillet over moderate heat, turning pieces carefully until fish is firm. Add liquid mixture and cook, stirring carefully until sauce is thick and clear. Add remaining ingredients; mix carefully. Cook until vegetables are heated and fish flakes easily when tested with a fork. Serve with rice.

TROUT CARIBBEAN

6 servings

2 pounds Trout fillets
½ cup Onion, chopped
1 cup Celery, chopped
½ cup Butter or Margarine, melted
¼ cup Parsley, chopped
1 Garlic Clove, crushed
½ Lemon
¼ teaspoon Thyme, powdered

1 Bay Leaf
¼ teaspoon Oregano, crushed
2 teaspoons Salt
Dash Pepper
3 cups (or 1 #2½ can)
   canned Tomatoes
3 cups cooked Rice

Cut trout into serving-size pieces, if necessary. Put onion and celery in a deep frying pan and cook until they are tender. Add all other ingredients except the fish and rice and simmer for 30 minutes. Remove chopped lemon, garlic and bay leaf. Place fish in the sauce and continue simmering for 30 minutes. Serve over cooked rice.

FRIED FISH WITH ONIONS

6 servings

2 pounds Fish fillets
¼ cup Flour
½ teaspoon Paprika
1¼ teaspoons Salt

½ cup melted Butter or Cooking Oil
4 Onions, thinly sliced
1 cup Cider Vinegar

Thaw fish, if frozen. Cut into serving portions. Combine flour and paprika and mix. Sprinkle fish with 1 teaspoon of salt. Roll fish in flour mixture. Heat one-fourth cup fat in a skillet and arrange fish in a single layer in pan. Fry over moderate heat for 4 or 5 minutes, or until fish are browned. Turn carefully and fry another 4 or 5 minutes. While fish are frying, cook onions in a second skillet in remaining fat until onions are limp. Add vinegar and remaining salt; simmer 10 minutes or until most of liquid has evaporated. Spoon onion mixture over fish and cook over low heat for 10 minutes or until fish flakes easily when fork tested.

Deep Fat Frying Tips

1. Fillets or smaller pieces of fish are the best form for deep fat frying.
2. Fish should be prepared for deep fat frying in the same basic manner as for pan frying, except the coating must be thicker to provide more protection from the hot oil.
3. A heavy, deep pan or French fryer is needed as well as a wire fry basket.
4. Fill the deep fat frying pan no more than half full of oil and heat the oil to 350°F.
5. Place one layer of fish in the basket, with each piece separated.
6. There will be some bubbling of the hot oil when the fish are placed in it, so lower the fry basket slowly.
7. A crust will form on the fish quite rapidly if the temperature of the oil is correct.
8. Fry the fish until the outside coating is a golden brown; this takes from 3 to 5 minutes.
9. Keep the oil clean of any loose pieces of breading or coating mix; the food debris will overcook or burn and give the oil an unpleasant flavor.
10. Remember that the temperature of the deep fat oil is 350°F and any water dropped into the oil will boil violently, causing hot oil to spatter beyond the pan.
11. Never put frozen fish in the hot oil until it has been thawed and dried of excess moisture.
12. Drain the cooked pieces of fish on paper towels or a rack intended for that purpose. Then keep them warm on a serving plate in the oven until they are to be served.

A typical recipe for deep fat frying for six persons will require the following ingredients:

2 to 3 pounds Fish, cut into serving size pieces	1 teaspoon Salt
¼ cup Milk	As desired Pepper
1 Egg, beaten	1½ cups Dry Bread or Cracker Crumbs or Cereal

The milk, egg, and seasonings are combined as a dip for the fish before it is coated with the dry bread crumbs or similar cereal-based food product.

CORNMEAL BATTER-DIPPED FISH

6 servings

2 pounds Fish fillets
½ cup Cornmeal
½ cup sifted Flour
1 teaspoon Salt
½ teaspoon Pepper

½ cup Milk
1 Egg, beaten
2 tablespoons melted Fat or
    Cooking Oil

Cut the fish into serving-sized portions. Combine the cornmeal, flour, salt, and pepper in a bowl. Add milk, egg, and fat or cooking oil. Stir until smooth. Dip the fish into the batter and let drain over bowl. Fry in deep hot fat (350°F.) for three to five minutes, until golden brown, turning once. Remove from fat and drain on paper towels. Keep the cooked fish warm until ready to serve.

DEEP FAT FRIED PINEAPPLE FRITTER FISH

6 servings

2 pounds Fish fillets
1 Egg, beaten
½ cup crushed Pineapple, drained
½ cup Milk

1⅓ cups Flour
¼ teaspoon Salt
2 teaspoons Baking Powder

Cut the fish into serving-size portions. Combine egg, crushed pineapple, and milk. Mix flour, salt, and baking powder. Blend the two mixtures together in a batter. Dip the fish in the batter and fry in deep fat at 350°F. until golden brown and fish flakes when fork tested. Drain and serve on paper towels.

CODFISH BALLS

6 servings

1½ cups pre-cooked, flaked fresh
    Codfish, or Salt Cod which has been
    soaked
2 cups Mashed Potatoes
2 Eggs, beaten

1 teaspoon Butter, melted
¼ teaspoon Salt
¼ teaspoon Pepper
½ cup Onions, chopped
½ cup Bread Crumbs

Combine the above ingredients and beat in a bowl until smooth and fluffy. Shape into balls and roll in dry bread or cracker crumbs. Fry in deep hot fat until browned. Serve while hot.

4 servings

1½ pounds Fish fillets

As desired Salt

As desired Pepper

¼ cup Flour

Batter:

¾ cup Flour

¼ cup Corn Starch

1 cup Water

Combine batter ingredients and stir quickly without working the batter too hard. In a heavy, deep skillet heat cooking oil to 350°F. The pan should be no more than one-half filled with oil. Cut the fish into serving size pieces and sprinkle with salt and pepper. Dust the fish evenly with flour and dip into the batter. Allow the excess batter to drain back into bowl. Fry the batter-dipped fish in the hot oil until lightly browned. Drain and serve with cooked rice and tempura sauce.

Tempura Sauce:

½ pint Dashinomoto soup

4 tablespoons Shoyu

4 tablespoons Sake, or Sherry Wine

Mix ingredients and bring to a boil. Then divide into small individual serving bowls for each diner. Dashinomoto can be obtained as an instant soup mix. It contains dried bonito and seaweed. Shoyu is a Japanese soy sauce. Both items can be purchased at stores offering foreign or other specialty foods.

Oven Frying Tips

Although oven-frying does not actually fry food in the true sense of the term, the result is similar.

1. Instead of a frying pan or skillet, use a shallow, well-greased baking dish or pan.
2. Cut the fish into serving-size portions.
3. Dip the fish pieces in salted milk and coat with crumbs.
4. Place the fish skin side down in a single layer in the greased baking dish.
5. Pour a small amount of fat or oil over the breaded fish.
6. Bake the fish in a very hot oven, at 500°F.
7. The cooking time for oven-frying of fish is not more than 10 to 15 minutes.
8. As with other frying techniques, the fish will be ready to serve when the outside is a golden brown and the flesh flakes easily when tested with a fork.

A basic recipe for oven-fried fish for 6 persons includes the following ingredients:

2 pounds Fish fillets	1½ cups dry Bread Crumbs
½ cup Milk	or Cereal
1 teaspoon Salt	¼ cup melted Fat or Cooking Oil

The milk and salt are combined and the fish dipped in the mixture. The fish is then rolled in the bread crumbs or similar cereal product. The melted fat or oil is poured over the fish.

OVEN-FRIED FISH AND CHIPS

6 servings

6 small Fish, pan-dressed	1 Egg, beaten
1 teaspoon Salt	¼ cup Milk
Dash Pepper	2 cups Potato Chips, finely crushed
1 cup Parsley, chopped	3 tablespoons melted Fat or
¼ cup Butter or Margarine, softened	Cooking Oil

Clean, wash, and dry fish. Sprinkle inside and out with salt and pepper. Mix parsley and butter thoroughly, then spread about one tablespoon of the parsley butter mixture inside each fish. Combine the egg and milk and dip each fish in the milk-egg mixture. Then roll fish in potato chip crumbs. Place the fish in a well-greased shallow pan or on a cooky sheet. Sprinkle any remaining potato chip crumbs over the top of fish. Spoon on melted fat. Place pan or sheet of fish in oven and bake at 500°F., for 15 to 20 minutes. Test fish flesh with fork to check doneness.

OVEN-FRIED SNAPPY SNAPPERS

6 servings

2 pounds Red Snapper fillets
1 Egg, beaten
2 tablespoons Worcestershire sauce
Dash Tabasco, or Hot Pepper Sauce

1½ cups fried Noodles, crushed
3 tablespoons melted Fat or
Cooking Oil

Cut fish into serving-size portions. Combine egg, Worcestershire sauce, and hot pepper sauce. Dip fish in egg mixture and roll in fried noodle crumbs. Place fish in well-greased shallow pan or on a cooky sheet. Spoon melted fat or cooking oil over the fish. Bake in a very hot oven, approximately 500°F., 10 to 15 minutes, or until fish flakes easily when fork tested.

OVEN-FRIED CHEESE MACKEREL

6 servings

2 pounds Mackerel fillets
1 Egg, beaten
¼ cup Milk
1 teaspoon Salt
Dash Pepper
¾ cup dry Bread Crumbs

½ cup process Cheddar Cheese,
grated
¼ cup Parsley, chopped
3 tablespoons melted Fat or Cooking
Oil

Cut fillets into serving-size portions and wipe dry. Combine egg, milk, salt, and pepper. Mix bread crumbs, cheese, and parsley. Dip fish in egg mixture and roll in crumb mixture. Place fish on a well-greased shallow pan or cooky sheet. Sprinkle any remaining crumb mixture over the top of fish. Spoon the melted fat or cooking oil over the fish. Bake in a very hot oven, about 500°F., for 10 to 15 minutes. Check fish doneness with a fork; it should flake easily when ready to serve.

POACHING AND
STEAMING FISH

POACHING FISH

Poaching is a method of cooking in a liquid at a temperature just under the boiling point of water. Lean fish usually are selected for poaching since the flesh holds together better than fat fish for this cooking method. A few of the fish species that can be handled well for poaching are carp, red snapper, sea bass, and whitefish. Whole fish, thick slices, or fillets can be used.

Poaching Tips
1. The objective in poaching is to keep the fish immersed in liquid so the size of the fish to be cooked will dictate the size of the pan used. For poaching a whole fish, a large skillet or a roasting pan can be used.
2. To keep the liquid from steaming away, have a tight-fitting lid on the pan.
3. Since poached fish are very delicate, it is helpful to have a way to lift them out of the liquid when they are cooked. Two ways in which this can be done are: (1) wrap the fish in a piece of cheesecloth before placing it in the pan, and (2) place the fish in a wire basket or on a rack which can be lowered into the fluid.
4. The liquid varies, depending on what flavor is desired. It can be, for example, water that has been slightly salted, or seasoned with spices and herbs, or mixed with white wine, or milk.
5. Generally, the fish is lowered into the already simmering liquid. However, in order to prevent the skin of a large whole fish from splitting, it is better to start with the fish in a cold liquid.
6. Timing, as always when cooking fish, is important. Again, never overcook. Simmer the fish at a rate of about 5 to 8 minutes per pound of fish, or until the fish flakes easily when fork tested.
7. Unless a Court Bouillion containing vinegar is used for the poaching liquid, it is frequently reduced and thickened to make a fish sauce.
8. Poached fish can then be served with this sauce, or some other preferred sauce. Poached fish can also be used flaked in many combination dishes such as casseroles, fish cakes, or salads.

BASS IN BOUILLON

6 servings

3 pounds Bass, whole, cleaned
1 quart Water
1 pint White Wine
1 tablespoon Vinegar
1 Onion, sliced

1 teaspoon Salt
Dash Pepper
1 spray Parsley
1 Bay Leaf

Combine water, wine, vinegar, onion, and seasonings in a roasting pan with a lid. Boil gently for about 15 minutes. Wrap the fish in cheesecloth and lower into the liquid in the pan, after boiling has ceased. Cook the fish in the liquid at a temperature of about 190°F. for 15 to 20 minutes. Watch temperature carefully so that fluid does not boil. Fork test a bit of the flesh to make sure fish is done. If ready, gently lift the fish in the cheesecloth from the liquid to a serving dish. Carefully remove the cheesecloth from the fish and garnish the fish with parsley, lemon slices, or other appropriate items.

SALMON WITH YOGURT SAUCE

4 servings

4 Salmon steaks
1 pint Water

1 Lemon, cut into thin slices
½ teaspoon Salt

Yogurt Sauce:
1 cup Plain Yogurt
1 Cucumber, chopped
2 tablespoons Chives, chopped

¼ teaspoon fresh Dill, minced
1 tablespoon Lemon Juice
½ teaspoon Salt

Add lemon slices and salt to water in deep pan or large skillet and bring the fluid to the boiling point. Then reduce heat below the boiling point, to 190 or 195°F., and lower fish steaks into pan or skillet on a rack or in a cheesecloth bag. Simmer for 10 to 15 minutes, until fish flakes easily when fork tested. When fish is ready, remove to a serving dish. Meanwhile, mix sauce ingredients in a bowl and serve with the poached fish steaks.

COD CURRY

6 servings

2 pounds fillets of Cod, or other white fish
1½ cups Apples, peeled and chopped
1 cup Onions, sliced
1 Garlic Clove, minced
3 tablespoons Butter or Margarine

4 teaspoons Flour
1 teaspoon Salt
1½ teaspoons Curry Powder
¼ teaspoon Powdered Ginger
1 (1 pound)can Tomatoes, with juice
6 servings cooked Rice

Thaw fish if frozen. Remove skin and bones. Cut fillets into pieces abut 1½ inches in size. Using a large skillet with a cover, cook the apples, onions, and garlic in butter or margarine until tender. Blend in the flour and seasonings. Then add tomatoes and mix thoroughly. Cover the mixture in the skillet and simmer for about 20 minutes, stirring occasionally. Add the fish, cover, and simmer 10 minutes more, or until fish flakes when fork tested. Serve on hot, cooked rice.

POACHED FISH IN WINE

6 servings

2 pounds Fish fillets
1 cup White Wine
2 tablespoons Dry Sherry
1½ tablespoons Lemon Juice
½ pound sliced Mushrooms
¼ cup Butter

2 Egg Yolks
1 cup Heavy Cream
1 tablespoon fresh Parsley, chopped
¾ teaspoon Salt
⅛ teaspoon Pepper

Poach fish in the wine, sherry, and lemon juice 5 to 10 minutes, or until fish flakes easily when fork tested. Carefully remove fish to a platter and keep warm in an oven until ready to serve. Continue cooking the fluid in which the fish was poached for about 10 minutes. In a separate pan, saute the mushrooms in 1 tablespoon of butter. In a bowl, beat the egg yolks and add cream. Pour the wine mixture into the egg yolks and cream combination, stirring constantly. Then add the remaining butter, parsley, salt and pepper, and the sauted mushrooms. Pour the sauce over the hot fish and serve.

2 pounds Fish fillets, any lean
   white Fish
2 cups boiling Water
1 teaspoon Salt
1 small Onion, sliced
¼ cup Lemon Juice
4 tablespoons Horseradish, freshly
   grated or prepared
1 pint Sour Cream
1 teaspoon Salt
⅛ teaspoon White Pepper
2 tablespoons Chives, finely
   chopped

1 teaspoon Rice Vinegar, or any
   White Vinegar
3 tablespoons fresh Dill, finely
   chopped
1 cup fresh Carrots, thinly sliced
1 cup Cucumbers, peeled and diced
2 tablespoons diced Pimiento
1 cup Celery, thinly sliced diagonally
1 head Boston Lettuce, or any
   crisp salad greens
2 Eggs, hard-cooked
3 fresh Tomatoes, peeled
   and sliced

Cut the fish fillets into 2-inch chunks and place the pieces in a large skillet. Add boiling water, 1 teaspoon of salt, onion, and lemon juice. Cover and simmer 5 to 10 minutes, or until the fish flakes easily when fork tested. Carefully remove the fish from the liquid and drain.

If prepared horseradish is used, first drain it. In a large bowl, combine the horseradish, sour cream, salt, pepper, chives, vinegar, and two tablespoons of the chopped dill. Carefully add the carrots, cucumbers, pimiento, celery and the cooked fish chunks to the horseradish dressing. Place the mixture in a refrigerator to chill for about 30 minutes. Arrange the fish, vegetables, and other dressing components on a bed of salad greens. Garnish with the sliced eggs and tomatoes. Sprinkle the remaining chopped dill over the salad and serve.

6 servings

3 pounds fresh Salmon	1 Celery stalk, chopped
1 teaspoon Salt	1 Bay Leaf

Egg Sauce:

2 tablespoons Butter or Margarine	½ teaspoon Salt
2 tablespoons Flour	¼ teaspoon Paprika
2 cups Milk	2 Eggs, hard-cooked

Add teaspoon of salt and chopped celery and bay leaf to boiling water in a deep pan or kettle. Turn down heat to simmering temperature and lower fish into the simmering liquid; the fish can be placed in a pie tin wrapped in cheese cloth for lowering into the hot water. Simmer the fish in the pan while it is covered for about 20 minutes. Then carefully lift fish out of the fluid and transfer it to a large heated serving dish.

Melt butter for the sauce and remove from heat. Add flour, stirring it into the butter until it is a smooth mixture. Gradually add milk to the mixture and return it to the heat. Cook about one minute, or until the mixture thickens. Add the seasonings and the sliced egg. Serve the sauce over the poached salmon.

STEAMING FISH

While poaching fish is a method of cooking it in a liquid, steaming is a technique in which a fish is supported out of and over a boiling liquid. The advantage of steaming is that the fish is able to retain its natural flavor when that is an objective.

Steaming Tips

1. There are cooking pans especially made for steaming. However, any large, deep pan with a tight cover can be used as long as an improvised rack is substituted for the tray. A colander, found in most kitchens, can be used as a fish tray for steaming. The objective here is to keep the hot liquid from actually touching the fish, and to allow steam to flow around it.
2. The water used for steaming may be merely salted or seasoned with spices, herbs, or wine. When it is suggested in a recipe that a certain amount of water be used, adjust the actual amount of water put into your own steamer pan so the surface of the liquid barely reaches the rack; never let the water level reach a depth that comes over the rack.
3. The water should be brought to a rapid boil so it is steaming heavily. The fish is then placed on the rack, which should be well-greased, and the pan is covered tightly. The heat can be reduced as long as the boiling continues.
4. Whole, dressed fish or fillets, steaks, and chunks of fish can be steamed. The usual practice is to steam large chunks with an even thickness. This simplifies the timing of the process.
5. Time the steam cooking as you would for poaching, that is, between 5 and 10 minutes per pound of fish, or until the fish flakes easily when tested with a fork. Rather than lose steam by repeated lifting of the lid to fork test the fish, make a considered estimate beforehand of the thickness of the fish. Then steam 5 minutes for the first ½ inch and several additional minutes for every other ½ inch of thickness.
6. Steamed fish are served in the manner of poached fish. Any skin or bones remaining on the fish after cooking should be removed. The meat can then be flaked for combination dishes such as casseroles or salads. Steamed fish also may be served in whole pieces, as they come from the steaming pan, and garnished or served with a sauce.

SIMPLE STEAMED FISH RECIPE

Makes 2 cups of cooked fish

1½ pounds Fillets, fresh or frozen,
   steaks, or pan-dressed fish

1 quart Water, boiling
1½ teaspoons Salt

Thaw fish, if frozen. Pour water into steamer pan, making sure it does not cover bottom of rack. Grease the rack well. Bring water temperature up to boiling. Place the fish on the rack and sprinkle with salt. Cover the pan and cook the fish over the boiling water for about 10 minutes, or until the flesh flakes easily when fork tested. Remove fish from pan and allow it to cool so that skin and bones, if any, can be removed. Flake the fish for any combination dish.

STEAMED TURBOT WITH AVOCADO DRESSING

6 servings

2 pounds Turbot chunks, steaks,
   or fillets
1 quart Water
1 teaspoon Salt
1 tablespoon Dried Dill weed
2 Avocado Pears

2 tablespoons Lemon Juice
As desired Salt
As desired Pepper
Pinch Cayenne Pepper
4 tablespoons Light Cream

Measure amount of water needed to fill pan to level just below steamer rack. Add salt and dill weed to the water. Wrap turbot in cheesecloth and place on greased rack in pan. Cover pan, bring water to rapid boil, and steam fish for 10 to 20 minutes, or until fish flakes easily when fork tested. Allow fish to cool and arrange on serving platter. Mash the peeled avocados with lemon juice and season to taste with salt, pepper, and cayenne. Stir in cream to desired consistency. Spread the avocado dressing smoothly over and around the turbot as you would spread frosting over a cake.

STEAMED CARP WITH CIDER SAUCE

3 to 4 pounds Carp, pan-dressed
3 cups Water
1 cup Apple cider
1 teaspoon Salt
¼ teaspoon Ginger
3 tablespoons Cornstarch

1 tablespoon Soy sauce
½ cup Green Onions, chopped
½ cup Green Pepper, finely chopped
½ cup Pineapple, drained and
  chopped

Combine water, cider, salt, and ginger in a pan for steaming. Wrap carp in cheesecloth and place the fish on a well-greased steamer rack in the pan, making sure the liquid does not touch the fish. Cover the pan and bring the cider mixture to a boil. Steam about 20 to 25 minutes, or until the fish flakes easily when tested with a fork.

Remove the fish from the pan and carefully separate it from the cheesecloth. Keep the fish warm on a heated platter until ready to serve. Reduce cider-water mixture to 2 cups. Soften cornstarch with a little cold water and stir it into the cider mixture. When it begins to thicken, add soy sauce, onion, green pepper, and pineapple. Cook until the green of the onion and pepper brightens. Pour the mixture over the carp and serve.

COLD TROUT WITH MUSTARD SAUCE

6 servings

6 Rainbow Trout, whole, cleaned
1 quart Water
1 teaspoon Dill, finely chopped
1 tablespoon Parsley, finely chopped

1 tablespoon Chives, finely chopped
1 Cucumber, peeled and sliced
3 Eggs, hard-cooked, sliced
Mustard Sauce*

Place trout on a rack over hot water so that water does not touch fish. Cover and steam until fish flakes when fork tested. Remove fish to a serving platter and chill thoroughly in a refrigerator. When fish are cold, strip skin carefully from sides of fish but leave heads and tails intact. Sprinkle the trout with dill, parsley, and chives. Arrange alternate slices of egg and cucumber on each fish. Serve with mustard sauce.

*Mustard Sauce (see p. 138)

FISH SOUFFLE

6 servings

2 cups Fish fillets, flaked,
   cooked (or about 1½ pounds
   steamed equivalent)
1 quart Water, boiling for steaming fish
¼ cup Celery, finely chopped

¼ cup Parsley, finely chopped
5 Egg Whites
2 tablespoons Bread Crumbs
1 tablespoon melted Butter
1 tablespoon Parmesan cheese, grated

Medium Cream Sauce:
(2 cups)
3 tablespoons Butter
3 tablespoons Flour
2 cups Light Cream

As desired Salt
As desired Pepper
4 Egg Yolks

Place fish fillets on a greased rack in a steamer. Pour in enough boiling water to bring the level up to but not over the fish rack. Cover the pan and steam the fish about 10 minutes, or until fish flakes easily when tested with a fork. Remove skin and bone if necessary and flake fish. Prepare Medium Cream Sauce: melt the butter and blend in the flour. Stir in the cream and season to taste. Remove from heat.

Beat the egg yolks and combine with the cream sauce. Add the flaked fish, celery, and parsley. Cool to a lukewarm temperature. Beat egg whites until stiff. Fold in the creamed fish mixture. Pour into greased six-cup size casserole. Combine crumbs, melted butter, and cheese, and sprinkle over top of casserole. Bake the souffle in a 350°F. oven for about 30 minutes, until firm.

MACKEREL-MACARONI SALAD

6 servings

1½ cups Flaked Mackerel
2 cups Shell macaroni, cooked
1 tablespoon Salad Oil
3 tablespoons Plain Yogurt
1 tablespoon Lemon Juice

1 cup chopped Celery
¼ cup Sweet Pickle, diced
¼ cup Cucumber, diced
½ Pimiento, cut fine
6 Green Peppers

Steam and flake mackerel. Cook and drain macaroni. Stir together the salad oil, yogurt, and lemon juice. Combine all ingredients except the peppers and chill. Make green pepper cups and when ready to serve, fill the peppers with the chilled salad.

STEAMED CREAMED SMOKED FISH IN PITA BREAD

6 servings

1½ pounds Smoked Fish fillets
1 quart Water, boiling
⅔ cup Sour Cream
1 teaspoon Lemon Juice
½ teaspoon Dried Dill Weed
½ teaspoon Salt

3 tablespoons Feta Cheese,
    crumbled (optional)
¼ cup Black Greek Olives,
    pitted and chopped
¼ cup Celery, finely chopped
6 pieces Pita Bread

Freshen smoked fish in cold water for at least one hour before cooking in a steamer. Drain and dry. Place smoked fillets on a greased steamer rack. Add only enough boiling water to reach bottom of rack without covering it. Cover the pan and steam the smoked fish four to five minutes for each one-half inch of thickness, or until fish flakes easily when fork tested. Remove fish, and allow it to cool. Remove skin and bones if needed, and flake.

Combine the flaked fish with the sour cream, lemon juice, dill weed, salt, feta cheese, olives, and celery. Chill in a refrigerator until ready to serve. To serve, warm the pita bread and open each piece to form a pocket. Stuff each piece of pita bread with creamed smoked fish.

SOLE ROLL-UPS IN ASPIC

6 servings

1½ pounds Sole fillets
¼ teaspoon Salt
1 to 2 pints Water, boiling, for steaming
1 tablespoon Gelatin
¼ cup canned Tomato Juice, cold

1½ cups hot Tomato Juice
1 teaspoon Lemon Juice
1 teaspoon Basil
As needed Salad Greens
As needed Tartar Sauce

Cut fillets into serving-size pieces. Sprinkle with salt. Roll and secure each with a toothpick. Place fish rolls on greased steamer rack above boiling water. Cover and steam five to ten minutes, or until fish flakes when tested. Soften gelatin in cold tomato juice. Combine with hot tomato juice, lemon juice, and basil. Chill and when it is about to set, pour into wet individual molds to one-third capacity. Place a fish roll-up into each mold, remove toothpick, cover with aspic. Chill until firm. Unmold on crisp greens and serve with tartar sauce

POMPANO PAPAYA

6 servings

1½ pounds Pompano fillets
As needed Water for steaming fish
3 ripe Papayas, halved, seeded

1 cup Mayonnaise (See sauces, p. 000)
1 teaspoon Curry Powder
⅓ cup Macadamia Nuts, chopped

Prepare mayonnaise sauce several days in advance. When ready to cook fish, stir curry powder into two to three tablespoons of the mayonnaise. Combine with the rest of the mayonnaise, stir thoroughly, and refrigerate until ready to serve. Place pompano on greased rack and cook over boiling water until tender, 10 or more minutes, depending on thickness of fish. When fish flakes easily, remove from steamer and allow it to cool. Then flake it into bite-sized pieces. Fill the cavities of the papayas with the flaked pompano. Stir a spoonful of curried mayonnaise in with the fish and top with a dollop of it. Sprinkle chopped nuts over each and serve with remaining mayonnaise.

MULLET REMOULADE

8 servings

1 pound Mullet fillets
As needed Water for steaming fish
2 tablespoons Olive Oil
2 tablespoons Tarragon Vinegar
½ teaspoon Salt
1 tablespoon prepared Mustard

1 teaspoon Paprika
½ teaspoon Horseradish
¼ cup Celery, chopped fine
1 Green Onion with top, chopped fine
1 tablespoon Parsley, minced
4 Grapefruit

Place fish on a greased rack over boiling water and cover; steam for about 10 minutes or until fish flakes easily. Remove fish, cool, and cut into bite-size pieces. Prepare remoulade sauce by mixing oil, vinegar, and salt. Add mustard, paprika, horseradish, celery, onion, and parsley, and mix thoroughly. Cut grapefruit into halves, remove core and part of pulp. Mix grapefruit pulp and mullet with remoulade sauce. Fill grapefruit shells with the mixture and serve chilled.

BROILING FISH

Many kinds of fish, fatty or lean, can be broiled. The fish can be in the form of whole, pan-dressed, steaks, or fillets. But thicker pieces, one inch thick or more, do best because the intense heat of the broiler has a drying effect on the fish flesh. Frozen fish should be thawed before the start of broiling.

Oven Broiling Tips
1. Follow the directions of the range manufacturer for preheating the broiler.
2. Oil the broiling pan or use aluminum foil.
3. Brush the fish well with oil, butter, or a basting sauce before cooking. Brush oil or fat or sauce once or twice again while the fish is broiling to help keep it moist.
4. If skin remains on the fish, dust it first with flour before applying oil or butter.
5. Fillets require more basting than whole fish.
6. Cooking time depends upon the thickness of the fish and the distance from the heat. A rule of thumb is to place the surface of the fish about 3 to 4 inches from the source of the heat.
7. Cooking time can range from 5 to 20 minutes, depending upon the size and thickness. Estimate about 5 minutes per ½ inch. Always test for the "flakes easily" sign of doneness.
8. In general, fillets and split fish do not need to be turned during broiling, but whole fish and thick steaks should be turned halfway through the cooking time. When turned they should be basted again.
9. Broiled fish should be served hot from the broiler, with a sauce of lemon.

BROILED FINNAN HADDIE

4 servings

2 pounds Finnan Haddie, or smoked Haddock	2 tablespoons melted Butter
1 quart hot water	As desired Pepper

Cover the finnan haddie with hot water. Soak for 10 minutes, then drain. Place the fish on a greased broiler rack. Brush on melted butter and sprinkle lightly with pepper. Preheat broiler, if needed. Broil under moderate heat, turning once, until fish is browned and flakes easily when fork tested.

BROILED HADDOCK IN HERB MARINADE

6 servings

2 to 3 pounds Haddock Steaks, 1 inch
  or more thick
2 Bay Leaves
½ teaspoon Thyme
¼ teaspoon Rosemary

1 Garlic Clove
1 cup White Wine Vinegar
3 tablespoons Cooking Oil or
  melted Butter

Combine bay leaves, thyme, rosemary, garlic, and white wine vinegar in a saucepan. Simmer 5 minutes to blend flavors. Cool and pour over fish in a shallow dish. Cover and let stand at least 30 minutes. Preheat broiler if needed. Drain haddock and place on greased broiler rack. Brush on cooking oil or melted butter. Broil under moderate heat, turning once and basting with butter or oil. When fish is browned and flakes easily it is done.

BROILED FLOUNDER WITH TOMATO AND CHEESE SAUCE

6 servings

2 pounds Flounder fillets
2 tablespoons Butter, melted
1 teaspoon Salt

1 (8-ounce) can Tomato Sauce
1 medium Onion, chopped
½ cup Cheddar Cheese, grated

Cut fillets into 6 portions. In well-greased broiler pan, arrange fillets and brush with melted butter. Sprinkle with salt. Place pan about 3 inches from the source of heat and broil about 8 minutes. Pour tomato sauce over broiled fish. Sprinkle with chopped onion and cheese. Then broil an additional four minutes to melt the cheese. But fork test to make sure it is done before serving.

BROILED BLUEFISH

6 servings

3 to 4 pounds Fresh Bluefish, whole   ½ teaspoon Mint
¼ cup Olive Oil   1 teaspoon Salt
2 tablespoons Lemon Juice   ¼ teaspoon Ground Black Pepper
½ teaspoon Basil   1 medium Onion, thinly sliced

Split the bluefish for broiling. Place skin side down in a well-greased broiler pan. Heat the olive oil, lemon juice, and seasonings together for 30 seconds to blend the flavors. Then brush the mixture on the fish. Broil about 10 minutes, or until fish is browned and flakes easily. Baste frequently during cooking. Serve with sauce from pan fish was cooked in.

BEER BROILED PIKE

6 servings

3 pounds Pike, cleaned and split   6 tablespoons Lemon Juice
4 tablespoons Butter, melted   ½ teaspoon Tarragon
As desired Salt   1 cup Beer
As desired Pepper

Place split pike in a greased broiler pan, skin side down. Sprinkle with salt, pepper, and some of the lemon juice. Brush on melted butter and place under broiler, about 6 inches from the heat. Mix remaining lemon juice with tarragon and beer. Broil pike while basting frequently with the lemon juice and beer mixture. Continue broiling and basting for about 10 minutes, depending on size of fish, until it flakes easily when fork tested.

SPICY CATFISH BROIL

6 servings

6 Catfish, skinned and pan-dressed	2 Garlic Cloves, finely chopped
¼ cup melted Butter or Cooking Oil	½ teaspoon Curry Powder
⅓ cup Steak Sauce	1 teaspoon Salt
2 tablespoons Catsup	¼ teaspoon Pepper
2 tablespoons Wine Vinegar	

Place catfish in a single layer in a shallow pan or dish. Combine the seasonings and other ingredients into a sauce. Pour the sauce over the catfish and let it stand for 30 minutes, turning once to make sure fish are properly covered with the sauce. Remove the fish and reserve the remaining sauce for basting.

Place fish on a greased broiler pan. Brush with sauce. Place pan so fish are about 3 inches from the source of heat and broil the fish for five to seven minutes, or until lightly browned. Brush the fish several times with the sauce. Turn them carefully and baste again. Broil an additional 5 to 7 minutes, basting twice. When fish are browned and flake easily they are ready to serve.

BROILED TROUT SCANDINAVIA

6 servings

6 Rainbow Trout	3 tablespoons Flour
As needed Flour for dredging	1½ cups Milk
2 to 3 tablespoons Cooking Oil	¼ cup Lemon Juice
2 tablespoons Butter	1 cup Blue Cheese, crumbled

Thaw trout, if frozen. Wash and wipe dry with paper towels. Dip the fish in the milk, then roll them in flour. Heat the cooking oil (or fat) in a flame-proof dish; oil should make a layer at least one-eighth of an inch deep. Add the trout and fry on one side over moderate heat until lightly browned. While trout is frying, melt the butter in a sauce pan. Stir in three tablespoons of flour and cook for several minutes. Stir in milk slowly and cook until sauce is smooth and thickened. Then stir in lemon juice and half of the blue cheese.

Drain and discard oil from fish dish. Pour the sauce over the trout and sprinkle the remaining blue cheese over them. Place the trout in the broiler, about six inches from the heat, and broil for five to six minutes, until cheese melts and fish flakes easily when tested. Garnish with lemon wedges.

6 servings

1 Mackerel, about 4 pounds	1 Mackerel Roe Yield
As desired Salt	12 Bacon strips
As desired Pepper	3 Tomatoes, cut in halves
½ teaspoon Paprika	
1 tablespoon Olive Oil or melted Butter	

Split and bone the mackerel. Place skin side up on greased broiler rack. Sprinkle with salt, pepper, and paprika. Brush with oil or melted butter and place about four inches from source of broiler heat. Broil about five to six minutes, turning fish carefully to brush lightly with oil or butter. Add roe and bacon strips and broil an additional five minutes. Add tomato halves, turn roe and bacon, and broil five minutes longer, or until fish flakes easily when fork tested.

FISH-ISH-KABOBS

6 servings

2 pounds Fillets, lean white Fish	1 Garlic Clove, minced
¼ cup Sesame Seed	1 tablespoon Soy Sauce
⅓ cup Salad Oil	12 small white Onions, cooked
3 tablespoons Lemon Juice	12 Cherry Tomatoes
1 tablespoon Honey	6 slices Bacon
¼ teaspoon Ground Ginger	½ pound medium Mushrooms

Cut fish fillets into one-inch cubes. In a frying pan over medium heat, toast sesame seeds until golden brown; stir frequently to prevent scorching. Set aside. In a mixing bowl, combine the oil, lemon juice, honey, ginger, garlic, and soy sauce. Add fish cubes, onions, and tomatoes. Stir mixture until well coated with the marinade. Cover and chill for several hours, stirring occasionally. Cut bacon into squares. Remove fish and vegetables from marinade and dip the mushrooms in the marinade to coat them lightly.

Using skewers, place alternately the pieces of fish, bacon squares, onions, tomatoes, and mushrooms, until skewers are filled. Place skewered kabobs in a greased broiler pan and broil about three inches from source of heat until browned on one side, or about five minutes. Then turn, baste with remaining marinade, and continue cooking until other side is browned. Spread sesame seeds on a serving platter and turn each skewer of kabobs in seed to coat them evenly before serving.

BROILED PERCH

6 servings

6 Freshwater Perch
½ cup dried Bread Crumbs
¼ cup minced Onion
4 tablespoons melted Butter

½ teaspoon Salt
⅛ teaspoon Pepper
1 teaspoon Fennel Greens, chopped

Split fish so they will lie flat; remove backbones. Wipe fish with a damp cloth and place them in a shallow greased broiler pan. Combine the bread crumbs and other ingredients and spread the mixture over the fish. Place the pan of fish about six inches from the heat and broil for about 15 minutes or until fish flakes easily when fork tested.

POLLOCK BROIL

6 servings

2½ pounds Pollock steaks,
fresh or frozen
¼ cup Butter, melted
⅓ cup Lemon Juice

½ teaspoon Marjoram
½ teaspoon Salt
¼ teaspoon Pepper

Thaw pollock, if frozen, before broiling. Combine all seasonings with lemon juice and melted butter in a saucepan. Heat for 30 seconds to blend flavors and brush the sauce over both sides of the steaks. Preheat the broiler, if needed, and place fish on greased broiler rack. Broil for 5 minutes, then baste both sides of fish again. Turn steaks and broil 4 or 5 minutes on second side; when steaks are browned and fish flakes easily, they are done.

6 servings

2 pounds Fish steaks, any kind	1 teaspoon Salt (optional: onion salt)
3 tablespoons Salad Oil	¼ cup Mayonnaise
2 tablespoons Lemon Juice	1 teaspoon Instant Coffee Granules
1 tablespoon Instant Coffee Granules	1 Egg White, beaten stiff

Place fish steaks in a shallow dish. Dissolve one tablespoon instant coffee solids in lemon juice; add salad oil and salt. Mix thoroughly and pour over fish. Marinate for 30 minutes, turning once to make sure all steak surfaces are coated. Remove the fish from the marinade but save the sauce. Place fish in broiler, preheated if necessary. While fish is cooking, combine 1 teaspoon of instant coffee granules with mayonnaise and beaten egg white. Stir mayonnaise and egg white together gently.

After fish steaks have broiled about 3 or 4 minutes on one side, turn them carefully and brush with the remaining marinade. Broil an additional 4 to 5 minutes and fork test to make sure fish is done. Spread coffee flavored mayonnaise-egg white mixture over the fish and continue broiling until the topping is a golden brown. Then serve while hot.

GRILLING FISH

Charcoal grilling, or barbecuing, is a dry heat method of cooking fish over hot coals. In recent years this has become a popular technique for cooking fish which, because of their tender flesh, can be prepared quickly and easily over a charcoal grill. Pan-dressed fish, fillets, and steaks are all suitable for charcoal grilling. If the fish to be used are frozen, they should be thawed first.

Fish Grilling Tips

1. Because fish flake easily as their cooking time nears completion, they should be placed in a well-greased, long-handled wire grill that is hinged so that fish can be held firmly in place during turning or removal without losing shape.
2. Since charcoal grilling is a dry-heat cooking method, thicker cuts of fish should be used as they tend to dry out less during cooking than thin cuts.
3. To insure that the result of grilling will be a juicy and flavorful fish, use a sauce that contains some fat and baste generously before and during the cooking process.
4. Fish should be placed about 4 inches from moderately hot coals for cooking; thick pieces can be placed a few inches farther from the coals.
5. Depending upon the thickness of the fish, cooking time should range between 10 and 20 minutes.
6. Never overcook fish. Since they contain no tough connective tissue, fish cook more quickly than other types of meat. Therefore, fish should be cooked only until it flakes easily when tested with a fork.

Outdoor Barbecue Grill Tips

1. Line the bottom of the fire bowl with heavy-duty aluminum foil. This gives fuel economy by reflecting heat while at the same time making it easier to clean the fire bowl later.
2. If the bottom of the fire bowl is not perforated, place a layer of gravel or crushed stones, ¼ to ⅜ of an inch in diameter, under the coals before starting the fire to give an even heat distribution while allowing the fire to "breathe." Use enough gravel to make the bed level out to the edge of the bowl.
3. Start the fire about 45 minutes before cooking is scheduled to begin.
4. Stack the charcoal briquets in a pyramid and soak lightly with an approved lighting fuel. Never use gasoline or other highly volatile fuels.
5. After allowing about 60 seconds for the fuel to soak into the coals, light them. Take necessary precautions when starting a charcoal fire; do not add fuel after fire has started.
6. When the surface of the briquets is covered with a gray ash, spread the coals evenly so that the layer of coals is slightly wider than the area of food to be cooked on the grill.
7. Wood chips can be added to the fire to give a pleasant smoky flavor to the fish. But use non-resinous woods such as those from fruit or nut trees; avoid evergreen woods.
8. Soak the wood chips in water for an hour before placing them on the hot coals. Add a few chips at a time. If the chips flame up, add more wet chips to keep fire smoky and slow burning.

BARBECUED FISH FILLETS

6 servings

2 pounds Fish fillets, fresh or frozen	1 (8 ounce) can Tomato sauce
¼ cup chopped Onion	2 tablespoons Lemon Juice
2 tablespoons chopped Green Pepper	1 tablespoon Worcestershire Sauce
1 Garlic Clove, finely chopped	1 tablespoon Sugar
2 tablespoons melted Butter or	2 teaspoons Salt
Cooking Oil	¼ teaspoon Pepper

Thaw fish, if frozen. Cook the onion, green pepper, and garlic in butter or cooking oil until tender. Add the remaining ingredients and simmer for 5 minutes, stirring occasionally. Let the mixture cool. Cut the fish into serving portions and place the pieces in a single layer in a shallow baking dish. Pour the sauce mixture over the fish and let it stand for 30 minutes, turning the fish once. Remove the fish and reserve the sauce for basting.

Place the fish in a well-greased, hinged, wire grill, or grills. Place the fish about 4 inches from moderately hot coals and cook for 5 to 8 minutes. Baste with sauce. Then, turn and cook the other side for 5 to 8 minutes, or until the fish flakes easily when fork tested.

PATIO CATFISH GRILL

6 servings

6 Catfish, skinned and pan-dressed	2 teaspoons Salt
¾ cup Butter or Margarine, melted	As needed Paprika
⅓ cup Lemon Juice	

Thaw fish, if frozen. Clean, wash, and dry fish. Combine butter, lemon juice, and salt into a sauce. Cut 6 pieces of heavy-duty aluminum foil, about 18 by 18 inches square. Grease the aluminum foil pieces lightly on one side and place about 2 tablespoons of sauce on each piece of foil. Place the fish in the sauce and top each fish with remaining sauce and sprinkle with paprika. Bring the foil up over the fish and close the edges to make 6 tightly closed packages. Place the packages on a barbecue grill about 6 inches from moderately hot coals. Cook the fish for 25 to 30 minutes, or until the fish flakes easily when tested with a fork.

ANCHOVY BUTTERED FISH STEAKS

6 servings

2 pounds Fish steaks
1 teaspoon Salt
Dash Pepper
3 tablespoons Butter or Margarine,
  melted
2 teaspoons Lemon Juice

1 teaspoon Anchovy paste
3 tablespoons Butter or other fat,
  melted
Dash Paprika
1 tablespoon chopped Parsley

Cut steaks into serving portions and sprinkle with salt and pepper. Place fish in greased, hinged, long-handled wire grills and brush with butter. Cook with fish steaks about 4 inches from moderately hot coals for 5 to 8 minutes, basting occasionally. Turn the fish and cook on other side for five to eight minutes, basting occasionally. Meanwhile, combine lemon juice, anchovy paste, butter, paprika, and parsley and mix thoroughly into a sauce. When fish steaks are cooked, remove from barbecue grill to serving dishes and coat them with the anchovy butter sauce.

GRILLED SMOKED FISH

6 servings

2 pounds Smoked Salmon or other
  smoked fish
2 tablespoons Butter of other fat,
  melted
Dash Pepper
2 tablespoons Butter or other fat

2 tablespoons Flour
1 cup Milk
½ teaspoon Salt
Dash Pepper
3 Eggs, hard-cooked

Place fish in well-greased, hinged, wire grill about 4 inches from moderately hot coals and cook for about 7 minutes. Turn, baste with butter and sprinkle with pepper. Grill for an additional 5 minutes or more. Meanwhile, melt 2 tablespoons of butter and blend in the flour. Add the milk and cook until thick and smooth, stirring constantly. Remove the yolk of one hard-cooked egg and reserve it for garnishing; chop the other eggs and mix with the flour, milk, fat and seasonings. When fish is cooked, serve it with the sauce and garnish with grated egg yolk.

FISH STEAKS EPICUREAN

6 servings

2 pounds Fish steaks	1 teaspoon Rosemary leaves
1 teaspoon Salt	2 tablespoons White Vinegar
Dash Pepper	2 tablespoons Salad Oil

Sprinkle both sides of the fish steaks with salt and pepper. Add rosemary and vinegar to the salad oil, shake well and let it stand at room temperature for at least 60 minutes; strain. Dip the fish in the oil mixture and place the fish in greased, hinged, wire grills. Set the wire grills about 3 to 4 inches from moderately hot coals and cook for 5 to 8 minutes. Baste the steaks with the oil mixture and turn carefully. Brush the other side with oil and cook 5 to 8 minutes more, basting occasionally with remaining oil mixture. When fish flakes easily, remove from heat and serve.

WHITEFISH IN FOIL

6 servings

2 pounds Whitefish fillets, fresh or frozen	2 tablespoons Lemon Juice
2 Green Peppers, sliced	2 teaspoons Salt
2 Onions, sliced	1 teaspoon Paprika
¼ cup Butter or Margarine, melted	Dash Pepper

Thaw fish, if frozen. Cut into serving-size portions. Cut 6 pieces of heavy-duty aluminum foil into 12 by 12 inch size pieces. Grease one side of aluminum foil. Place a portion of fish, skin side down, on each piece of foil and top with slices of green pepper and onion. Combine the other ingredients into a sauce and pour over the fish pieces. Bring the foil up over the fish chunks and close the edges with tight double folds. Place the 6 packages of fish on a charcoal grill about 5 inches from moderately hot coals. Cook for 45 to 60 minutes, or until fish flakes easily when fork tested.

YELLOW PERCH DELIGHT

6 servings

2 pounds Yellow Perch, pan-dressed　　¼ teaspoon Pepper
2 tablespoons Lemon Juice　　　　　　　1 pound sliced Bacon
2 teaspoons Salt

    Thaw fish, if frozen. Clean, wash, and dry fish. Brush the inside of the fish with the lemon juice and sprinkle with salt and pepper. Wrap the fish in slices of bacon and place the bacon-wrapped fish in well-greased, hinged wire grills. Set the grills about 5 inches from moderately hot coals and cook for about 10 minutes. Then turn the grills and cook the other side for 10 to 15 minutes, or until bacon is crisp and fish flakes easily when tested with a fork.

CAMPFIRE SMELT

6 servings

3 pounds Smelt, pan-dressed　　　⅓ cup chopped Onion
2 teaspoons Salt　　　　　　　　　⅓ cup chopped Parsley
Dash Pepper　　　　　　　　　　　3 strips of Bacon, cut in halves

    Thaw fish, if frozen. Clean, wash, and dry on paper towels. Cut 6 pieces of heavy-duty aluminum foil into 12 by 12 inch size pieces. Grease the foil lightly and divide fish into 6 equal portions on pieces of foil. Sprinkle with salt and pepper. Place onion and parsley pieces on fish and top with bacon. Bring the foil up over the fish and close the edges with tight double folds. Place the 6 packages on a charcoal grill about 4 inches from hot coals. Cook for 10 to 15 minutes, or until the fish flakes easily when tested with a fork.

SESAME RAINBOW TROUT

6 servings

6 Rainbow Trout, pan-dressed	2 tablespoons Lemon Juice
¼ cup melted Fat or Cooking Oil	½ teaspoon Salt
¼ cup Sesame Seeds	Dash Pepper

Thaw fish, if frozen. Clean, wash, and dry fish on paper towels. Place fish in well-greased, hinged, wire grills. Combine fat or oil, sesame seeds, lemon juice, and seasonings into a sauce. Baste fish with the sesame sauce. Place the fish about 4 inches from moderately hot coals and cook for 8 minutes. Baste again with sesame sauce. Turn and cook for another 7 to 10 minutes, or until fish flakes easily when fork tested.

FISH STEAKS ITALIAN STYLE

6 servings

2 pounds Fish steaks	2 teaspoons Salt
2 cups Italian Dressing	¼ teaspoon Pepper
2 tablespoons Lemon Juice	As needed Paprika

Thaw fish, if frozen. Cut into serving-size pieces and place in a single layer in a shallow baking dish. Combine Italian dressing, lemon juice, salt and pepper and mix thoroughly. Pour the mixture over the fish and let stand for 30 minutes, turning once. Remove fish, reserving sauce for basting. Place fish in well-greased, hinged wire grills. Sprinkle with paprika. Set grills about 4 inches from moderately hot coals and cook for about 8 minutes. Baste with sauce and sprinkle with paprika again. Turn and cook an additional 7 to 10 minutes, or until fish flakes easily when tested with a fork.

6 servings

2 pounds Swordfish steaks, or other fish steaks
¼ cup Orange Juice
¼ cup Soy Sauce
2 tablespoons Catsup
2 tablespoons melted Fat or Cooking Oil

2 tablespoons chopped Parsley
1 tablespoon Lemon Juice
1 Garlic Clove, finely chopped
½ teaspoon Oregano
½ teaspoon Pepper

Thaw steaks, if frozen. Cut into serving-size portions and place in a single layer in a shallow baking dish. Combine all the other ingredients and mix thoroughly into a sauce. Pour the sauce over the fish and let it stand for 30 minutes, turning once. Remove the fish and reserve the sauce for basting.

Put the fish into well-greased, hinged, wire grills and cook about 4 inches above moderately hot coals for approximately 8 minutes. Baste with the sauce. Then turn and cook for another 7 to 10 minutes, or until the fish flakes easily when tested with a fork.

STRIPED BASS SUPREME

6 servings

2 pounds Striped Bass fillets
½ cup melted Fat or Cooking Oil
½ cup Sesame Seeds
⅓ cup Cognac

⅓ cup Lemon Juice
3 tablespoons Soy Sauce
1 teaspoon Salt
1 large Garlic Clove, crushed

Thaw fillets, if frozen. Cut into equal serving portions and place in a single layer in a shallow baking dish. Combine the remaining ingredients into a sauce and pour the sauce over the fish fillets. Let stand for 30 minutes, turning once. Remove fish but reserve the sauce for basting. Place the fish fillets in well-greased, hinged, wire grills. Set the grills about 4 inches from moderately hot coals and cook for 8 minutes. Baste with the sauce. Turn and cook for an additional 7 to 10 minutes, or until fish flakes easily when tested with a fork.

6 servings

2 pounds Pickerel fillets, or other
   fish fillets
⅓ cup Soy Sauce
2 tablespoons melted Fat or Cooking Oil

1 tablespoon Liquid Smoke
1 Garlic Clove, chopped
½ teaspoon Ginger

Thaw fillets, if frozen. Cut into equal serving portions and place them in a single layer in a shallow baking dish. Combine the other ingredients into a sauce and pour the sauce over the fish. Let it stand for 30 minutes, turning once. Remove fish while reserving sauce for basting. Place fish in well-greased, hinged, wire grills and set grills about 4 inches above moderately hot coals. Cook for about 8 minutes, then baste with the sauce, turn and cook for an additional 7 to 10 minutes, or until the fish flakes easily when tested with a fork.

YELLOW PERCH KABOBS

6 servings

2 pounds Yellow Perch fillets
⅓ cup French Dressing
3 large fresh Tomatoes
1 (16-ounce) can whole Potatoes,
   drained

1½ teaspoons Salt
Dash Pepper
⅓ cup melted Fat or Cooking Oil

Thaw fillets, if frozen. Skin fillets and cut into strips about 1 inch wide and 4 inches long. Place fish strips in a shallow baking dish, then pour French dressing over them and let stand for 30 minutes. Wash tomatoes, remove stem ends, and cut into sixths. Remove fish and reserve dressing for basting. Roll the fish strips and place on skewers alternately with tomatoes and potatoes until skewers are filled.

Place kabobs in well-greased, hinged, wire grills. Add salt and pepper and remaining dressing to the melted fat or cooking oil and mix thoroughly. Baste the kabobs with the seasoned fat. Place the kabobs about 4 inches from moderately hot coals and cook for about 5 minutes. Baste with sauce, turn, and cook for 4 to 6 minutes longer, or until fish flakes easily when tested with a fork.

6 servings

6 Pan-dressed Flounder
Crab stuffing (see below)
¾ cup Butter or Margarine, melted

⅓ cup Lemon Juice
2 teaspoons Salt
As needed Paprika

Crab Stuffing:

1 pound Crab meat, fresh or frozen,
  or canned
½ cup Onion, chopped
⅓ cup Celery, chopped
⅓ cup Green Pepper, chopped
2 Garlic Cloves, chopped

⅓ cup melted Fat or Cooking Oil
2 cups Soft Bread Crumbs
3 Eggs, beaten
2 teaspoons Salt
1 tablespoon Parsley, chopped
½ teaspoon Pepper

Thaw crab meat, if frozen; drain crab meat, if canned. Remove any remaining shell or cartilage from crab meat. Cook onion, celery, green pepper, and garlic in fat until tender. Combine bread crumbs, eggs, salt, parsley, pepper, cooked vegetables, and crab meat. Mix thoroughly. Thaw flounder, if frozen. Clean, wash, and dry fish. Make a pocket for stuffing in each fish by laying the fish flat on a cutting board, light side down. With a sharp knife, cut down the center of the fish along the backbone from the tail to a point about 1 inch from the head end. Turn the knife flat and cut the flesh along both sides of the backbone to the tail, allowing the knife blade to run over the rib bones.

Stuff the fish loosely with crab mixture. Then combine the butter, lemon juice, and salt. Cut six pieces of heavy-duty aluminum foil into 18 by 18 inch squares. Grease foil squares lightly. Place 2 tablespoons of the lemon-butter sauce on the foil, then place fish in sauce. Top each fish with 1 tablespoon of sauce and sprinkle with paprika. Bring foil up over the fish and close the edges with tight double folds. Place the 6 foil packages on a barbecue grill about 6 inches from moderately hot coals and cook for 25 to 30 minutes, or until fish flakes easily when fork tested.

6 servings

2 pounds Lake Trout fillets
¼ cup French Dressing
1 tablespoon Lemon Juice

1 tablespoon grated Onion
2 teaspoons Salt
Dash Pepper

Thaw fillets, if frozen. Cut into serving portions and place in well-greased, hinged, wire grills. Combine remaining ingredients into a sauce and baste the fillets with it. Place fillets about 4 inches from moderately hot coals and cook for approximately 8 minutes. Baste again with sauce. Turn and cook for 7 to 10 minutes longer, or until fish flakes easily when tested with a fork.

6 servings

2 pounds Fish steaks, fresh or frozen	1 Garlic Clove, finely chopped
1 cup Dry Vermouth	¼ teaspoon Marjoram
¾ cup melted Fat or Cooking Oil	¼ teaspoon Pepper
⅓ cup Lemon Juice	¼ teaspoon Thyme
2 tablespoons Chives, chopped	⅛ teaspoon Sage
2 teaspoons Salt	⅛ teaspoon Liquid hot pepper sauce

Thaw fish steaks, if frozen. Cut into equal serving portions and place in a single layer in a shallow baking dish. Combine the remaining ingredients and mix thoroughly into a sauce. Pour the sauce over the fish and let stand 4 hours, turning occasionally. Remove fish and reserve sauce for basting. Place the fish in well-greased, hinged, wire grills. Set the grills about 4 inches from moderately hot coals and cook for approximately 8 minutes. Baste with sauce, then turn and cook for 7 to 10 minutes, or until fish flakes easily when tested with a fork.

6 servings

2 pounds Cod fillets, or other fish fillets	1 (8 ounce) can Tomato Sauce
2 tablespoons chopped Onion	2 tablespoons Sherry Wine
1 Garlic Clove	½ teaspoon Salt
2 tablespoons melted Fat or Cooking Oil	¼ teaspoon Oregano
	3 drops Liquid Hot Pepper Sauce
	Dash Pepper

Thaw fillets, if frozen. Cut fillets into serving portions and place them in a shallow baking dish. Cook chopped onion and garlic in fat until tender. Add remaining ingredients and simmer for 5 minutes, stirring occasionally. Cool mixture and pour over fish fillets and let stand for 30 minutes, turning once. Remove fish and reserve sauce for basting. Place fish in well-greased, hinged, wire grills and cook for about 8 minutes with fish about 4 inches from moderately hot coals. Baste with sauce. Turn and cook another 7 to 10 minutes, or until fish flakes easily when fork tested.

CHARCOAL GRILLED SNAPPER STEAKS

6 servings

2 pounds Red Snapper, or other
fish steaks
½ cup melted Fat or Cooking Oil
¼ cup Lemon Juice
2 teaspoons Salt

½ teaspoon Worcestershire Sauce
¼ teaspoon White Pepper
Dash Liquid Hot Pepper
Dash Paprika

Thaw steaks, if frozen. Cut into serving portions and place in well-greased, hinged, wire grills. Combine the remaining ingredients, except the paprika, into a sauce. Coat the fish steaks with the sauce and sprinkle with paprika. Place the wire grills about 4 inches from moderately hot coals and cook the fish for about 8 minutes. Baste with sauce and sprinkle with paprika; turn and cook for an additional 7 to 10 minutes, basting occasionally with remaining sauce. When fish flakes easily, remove from heat and serve.

GRILLED HALIBUT STEAKS

6 servings

2 pounds Halibut steaks
1 teaspoon Salt

Dash Pepper
¼ cup Butter or Margarine, melted

Cut fish steaks into serving portions and sprinkle with salt and pepper. Place steaks in well-greased, hinged, wire grills and set them about 4 inches from the hot coals of a barbecue grill. Brush the steaks with butter and cook for 5 to 8 minutes, or until one side is slightly brown. Baste with butter and turn carefully. Brush other side with butter and broil an additional 5 to 8 minutes, or until the fish flakes easily.

BAKING FISH

Baking, a form of dry-heat cooking, is one of the most popular and easiest cooking methods for fish. Fatty fish generally respond better to baking recipes than lean fish, but lean fish also can be baked if the cook remembers to keep the fish moist with a basting sauce.

Baking Tips

1. A good general rule is to preheat the oven, set at a moderate 350 degrees Fahrenheit.
2. As always, a fish should be cooked only until the flesh pulls away easily from the bones and flakes when tested with a fork. The time for baking a fish usually averages between 25 and 30 minutes for pan-dressed fish, fillets, or steaks and longer for whole fish. Stuffed fish also require a longer baking time.
3. Frozen fish can be baked without being thawed first, but cooking times must be longer.
4. To prepare a fish for baking, the head and tail can be removed or left intact as preferred. If the fish is split and boned, the skin should be left intact for stuffing.
5. The fish should be rinsed and dried and placed in a greased baking pan. The fish also should be basted with melted fat or oil to keep the surface moist, or covered with a sauce or topping such as bread crumbs.
6. If a fish is not going to be stuffed or baked with a sauce, both the outside and the body cavity should be brushed with a seasoned butter sauce. For a 3 pound fish, about ¼ cup of melted butter or margarine with 1 teaspoon of salt and ⅛ teaspoon of pepper would be recommended. An herbed butter also can be used.
7. In preparing stuffing for a fish, a rule of thumb is to use about 3 cups of stuffing for a 3-pound dressed fish, or approximately 1 cup of stuffing per pound. A basic baked fish recipe follows:

BAKED STUFFED FISH

6 servings

1 dressed Fish, about 3 pounds	¼ cup melted Fat or Oil
1 teaspoon Salt	3 cups Bread Stuffing
⅛ teaspoon Pepper	

Thaw fish, if frozen. Clean, wash, and dry fish. Sprinkle inside with salt and pepper. Place fish on a well-greased bake-and-serve platter, about 12 by 18 inches. Stuff fish loosely. Brush fish with fat or oil. Bake in a moderate oven at 350°F., for 45 to 60 minutes, or until the fish flakes easily when tested with a fork.

OCEAN PERCH BAKED IN SPANISH SAUCE

6 servings

2 pounds Ocean Perch fillets
¼ cup chopped Onion
3 tablespoons Butter or Margarine, melted
2 tablespoons Flour
2 cups canned Tomatoes

¼ cup chopped Green Pepper
1 teaspoon Salt
½ teaspoon Sugar
Dash Pepper
1 Bay Leaf
1 whole Clove

Cook onion in butter until tender. Blend in flour. Add the remaining ingredients except fillets and cook until thick, stirring constantly. Remove bay leaf and clove. Arrange fillets in a well-greased shallow baking dish and cover with a sauce. Bake in a moderate oven at 350°F., for 25 to 30 minutes, or until fish flakes easily when fork tested.

BAKED SMELTS ITALIAN STYLE

6 servings

2 pounds dressed Smelts
2 cups Onion, sliced
2 Garlic Cloves, minced
¼ cup melted Fat or Oil
1 (28-ounce) can Italian Tomatoes, undrained
1 (6 ounce) can Tomato Paste

1½ teaspoons Oregano
1½ teaspoons Salt
1 teaspoon Sugar
¼ teaspoon Pepper
¼ cup chopped Parlsey
1 cup Mozzarella Cheese, shredded
¼ cup Parmesan Cheese, shredded

Cook onion and garlic in melted fat or oil until onion is tender. Add tomatoes, tomato paste, oregano, 1 teaspoon salt, sugar, and pepper; mix well. Cover and cook slowly, about 30 minutes, until flavors are blended and mixture is slightly thickened; stir often while cooking. Stir in parsley.

Spread sauce over bottom of two to three quart shallow baking dish. Arrange smelt in a single layer on sauce down the center of the baking dish. Sprinkle with cheese and remaining one-half teaspoon of salt. Bake in a hot oven, at 400°F., for 15 to 20 minutes, or until fish flakes easily when fork tested.

6 to 8 servings

1 Rockfish, 3 to 4 pounds, dressed	4 cups Soft Bread Cubes
2½ teaspoons Salt	4 cups Spinach leaves, washed
1½ cups Celery, thinly sliced	and drained
¼ cup Green Onions, sliced	1 tablespoon Lemon Juice
½ cup Butter or Margarine, melted	¼ teaspoon Pepper

Thaw fish if frozen; clean, wash, and dry fish. Sprinkle inside and outside with one and a half teaspoons of salt. Cook celery and green onions in 6 tablespoons of butter or margarine until celery is tender. Stir in bread cubes and spinach leaves. Cook and stir until spinach is tender. Add lemon juice, remaining 1 teaspoon of salt, and pepper; toss lightly. Stuff fish loosely and close opening with small skewers. Place fish in a well-greased baking pan. Brush with remaining butter or margarine. Bake in a moderate oven, 350°F., for 40 to 60 minutes, or until fish flakes easily when tested with a fork.

6 servings

6 Rainbow Trout, pan-dressed	⅔ cup Green Onions, sliced
2 teaspoons Salt	¼ cup chopped Parsley
4 cups Soft Bread Cubes	2 tablespoons chopped Pimiento
⅔ cup Butter or Margarine	4 teaspoons Lemon Juice
1 cup sliced fresh Mushrooms	½ teaspoon Marjoram

Thaw fish, if frozen; clean, wash, and dry. Sprinkle 1½ teaspoons of salt evenly inside and outside of fish. Sauté bread cubes in one-half cup of butter or margarine until lightly browned, stirring frequently. Add mushrooms and onions; cook until mushrooms are tender. Stir in remaining salt, parsley, pimiento, lemon juice, and marjoram; toss lightly.

Stuff fish and arrange in a single layer in a well-greased baking pan. Brush with remaining melted butter or margarine. Bake in a moderate oven, 350°F., for 25 to 30 minutes, or until fish flakes easily when tested with a fork. Serve plain or with a fish sauce.

6 servings

2 pounds Fish fillets	¼ cup Dry White Wine
½ cup Celery, thinly sliced	2 tablespoons Flour
2 tablespoons Green Onions, sliced	1 cup "Half and Half"
⅓ cup Butter or Margarine	(milk and cream)
2 cups Soft Bread Crumbs	1 Egg Yolk, beaten
¼ teaspoon Tarragon leaves	1 cup cooked Shrimp
1¼ teaspoons Salt	1 teaspoon Lemon Juice
⅛ teaspoon White Pepper	

Thaw fish fillets, if frozen. Sauté celery and onion in 2 tablespoons butter or margarine until tender, but not browned. Stir in bread crumbs, tarragon leaves, ¼ teaspoon salt, and pepper. Divide fillets into serving portions and sprinkle fillets with ¾ of a teaspoon of salt. Cover each fillet with an equal amount of bread mixture. Then roll fillets and secure with wooden tooth picks or metal skewers.

Place rolled fillets in a shallow baking dish and drizzle with wine and 2 tablespoons of melted butter or margarine. Bake in a moderate oven at 350°F., for about 25 minutes, or until the fish flakes easily when fork tested. Baste with pan juices several times during cooking. Pour shrimp sauce over roll-ups and serve.

Shrimp Sauce:

Melt remaining butter or margarine in small saucepan; blend in flour and remaining ¼ teaspoon of salt. Stir in cream-milk mixture (or fresh milk); cook, stirring constantly, until thick and smooth. Fold a small amount of hot mixture into egg yolk, then stir egg yolk mixture into remaining sauce. Add shrimp, lemon juice, and pan juices to sauce, blending carefully. Heat to serving temperature before pouring over fish.

6 servings

6 Bullheads, skinned and pan-dressed	12 Lemon Slices
½ cup French Dressing	As desired Paprika

Thaw fish, if frozen. Clean, wash, and dry fish. Brush fish inside and out with French dressing. Cut six of the lemon slices in half and place 2 half slices in each body cavity. Place fish in a well-greased baking dish, about 10 by 14 inches in size, and brush tops of fish with remaining dressing. Top with a lemon slice on each fish and sprinkle with paprika. Bake in a moderate oven, 350°F., for 30 to 35 minutes, or until fish flakes easily when fork tested.

BAKED PERCH AND EGGS

1 pound Perch fillets
½ teaspoon Salt
½ cup Chili Sauce
6 Eggs, separated

½ teaspoon Salt
Dash Pepper
¼ teaspoon Paprika

Skin fillets and place in a well-greased, shallow baking dish. Sprinkle with salt and cover with chili sauce. Bake in a moderate oven, 350°F., for 20 to 25 minutes, or until fish flakes easily when tested with a fork. Beat egg whites until stiff but not dry; add seasonings. Spread on fish and top with slightly beaten egg yolks. Continue baking for 8 to 10 minutes, or until egg mixture is set. Garnish and serve.

STUFFED SEA BASS

6 to 8 servings

1 Dressed Sea Bass, about 4 pounds
1½ teaspoons Salt
1½ cups Celery, diced
1½ cups Onion, chopped
1 Garlic Clove, minced
1 Bay Leaf, crumbled

½ cup Butter or Margarine
4 cups Soft Bread Crumbs
2 tablespoons Parsley, chopped
½ teaspoon Rosemary
Dash Pepper

Thaw fish, if frozen; clean, wash, and dry. Sprinkle 1 teaspoon salt over inside of body cavity of fish and place in well-greased baking pan. Cook celery, onion, garlic, and bay leaf in ⅓ cup of butter or margarine until vegetables are tender. Add remaining salt, bread crumbs, parsley, rosemary, and pepper; toss lightly. Stuff fish loosely and brush with remaining butter or margarine. Cover fins and tail loosely with foil. Bake in a moderate oven, at 350°F., for 45 to 60 minutes, or until fish flakes easily when tested with a fork.

FISH AND VEGETABLE PIE

6 servings

2 cups Fish Flakes
2 tablespoons Butter or Margarine
2 tablespoons Flour
¼ teaspoon Salt

Dash Pepper
1 can Concentrated Vegetable Soup
½ can Water
1 cup Biscuit Mix

Melt butter, blend in flour and seasonings. Add soup and water and cook until mixture is thick, stirring constantly. Add fish. Pour into well-greased casserole dish. Prepare biscuit mix according to manufacturer's instructions. Cover fish and vegetable mixture with a layer of the biscuit mix. Bake in a hot oven, about 450°F., for 20 to 25 minutes, or until biscuit covering is brown.

DEVILED PIKE

6 servings

2 pounds Pike fillets
1½ teaspoons Salt
Dash Pepper
1 tablespoon Prepared Mustard

¼ cup Chili Sauce
3 tablespoons Onion, chopped
¼ teaspoon Worcestershire Sauce

Skin fillets and sprinkle with salt and pepper. Roll each fillet and fasten with toothpicks. Place rolled fillets in a well-greased baking pan. Combine remaining ingredients and spread on top of fish rolls. Bake in a moderate oven at 350°F., for 25 to 30 minutes, or until fish flakes easily when tested with a fork. Garnish with lemon wedges and serve.

BAKED SALMON ORIENTAL

6 servings

2 pounds Salmon steaks
2 teaspoons Salt
Dash Pepper
½ cup Flour
½ cup Butter or Margarine,
    melted

2 cups Celery, chopped
1 cup Onion rings
3 tablespoons Green Pepper,
    chopped
2 cups whole-kernel corn
2 tablespoons Soy Sauce

Sprinkle salmon steaks on both sides with 1 teaspoon of salt and dash pepper. Roll in flour and brown steaks quickly in melted fat. Place the browned steaks in a large, well-greased casserole dish. Cook celery, onion, and green pepper in the remaining fat until almost tender. Sprinkle with remaining salt and cover dish. Bake in a moderate oven at 350° for 25 to 30 minutes. Serve from casserole.

GREEN PEPPERS STUFFED WITH FISH

6 servings

2 pounds Fish fillets
6 large Green Peppers
6 tablespoons diced Bacon
3 tablespoons chopped Onion
¼ cup chopped Celery
¼ cup Chili Sauce

1 teaspoon Salt
Dash Pepper
2 tablespoons Butter or Margarine,
  melted
½ cup dry Bread Crumbs

Skin fish fillets and cut into ½ inch pieces. Cut a thin slice from the top of each green pepper and remove the seeds. Simmer peppers in boiling salted water for 10 to 12 minutes, or until almost tender. Drain. Fry bacon until crisp; add onion, celery, chili sauce, seasonings, and fish. Simmer about 10 minutes or until fish flakes easily when fork tested. Fill peppers with fish mixture. Combine butter and crumbs and sprinkle over top of peppers. Place stuffed peppers in a well-greased baking pan and bake in a moderate oven, at 350°F., for 20 to 25 minutes. Garnish and serve hot.

CORNBREAD STUFFED POLLOCK

6 servings

2 pounds Pollock or other fish fillets
1 cup sliced Celery
1 cup fresh Mushrooms, sliced
¼ cup Green Onions, sliced
½ cup Butter or Margarine
4 cups Cornbread, crumbled

2 cups Soft Bread Cubes
1¼ teaspoons Salt
½ teaspoon Fines herbes blend
½ cup hot Water
2 tablespoons Lemon Juice

Thaw fish fillets, if frozen. Cut fillets into equal serving portions. Add celery, mushrooms, and onions to 6 tablespoons butter or margarine in a 10-inch skillet. Cook until tender but not browned. Combine with ¼ teaspoon salt, fines herbes, and hot water; mix carefully. Toss lightly with breads. Turn stuffing into a well-greased baking dish, about 12 by 8 inches, and arrange fish in a single layer on stuffing.

Melt remaining two tablespoons of butter or margarine and drizzle over fish. Then sprinkle lemon juice over fish. Season with paprika and remaining one teaspoon of salt. Bake in a moderate oven, at 350°F., for 25 to 30 minutes, or until fish flakes easily when tested with a fork.

NEW ORLEANS CATFISH BAKE

6 servings

2 pounds Catfish steaks
½ teaspoon Salt
Dash Pepper
2 cups cooked Rice
2 tablespoons grated Onion

½ teaspoon Curry Powder
6 Lemon slices
¼ cup Butter or Margarine
As desired chopped Parsley

Thaw fish, if frozen. Cut into serving-size portions and place in a well-greased baking dish, about 10 by 14 inches in size. Sprinkle fish with salt and pepper. Combine rice, onion, and curry powder and spread mixture over fish. Top with lemon slices and dot with butter. Cover dish and place in a moderate oven, about 350°F., for 25 to 35 minutes, or until fish flakes easily when fork tested. Remove the baking dish cover for the last few minutes of cooking to allow for a light browning of fish. Sprinkle with chopped parsley and serve.

CHEESE CRUSTED FISH STEAKS

6 servings

2 pounds Fish steaks, fresh or frozen
½ cup Commercial Garlic and
  Herb dressing

½ cup Corn Flakes, finely crushed
½ cup Cheddar Cheese, shredded
6 Tomato slices

Thaw fish, if frozen. Cut steaks into serving portions and place in a single layer in a baking dish about 8 by 12 inches in size. Pour dressing over fish and place in a refrigerator for several hours, turning fish several times. Combine corn flake crumbs and cheese and roll fish in the mixture.

Arrange fish in a single layer in a well-greased baking dish, about 8 by 12 inches in size. Sprinkle any remaining crumbs-and-cheese mixture over the fish. Bake in a very hot oven, 450°F., for 15 to 20 minutes, or until fish flakes easily when tested with a fork. Garnish with tomato slices and serve.

6 servings

2 pounds Pollock fillets
1 cup chopped Onions
1 Garlic Clove, minced
2 tablespoons Butter or Margarine
1 (27-ounce) can Sauerkraut, drained
¼ cup Dry White Wine
¼ cup Water

½ teaspoon Caraway Seeds
1 teaspoon Salt
¼ cup Flour
¼ cup melted Fat or Cooking Oil
1 cup Sour Cream
½ cup Cheddar Cheese, shredded
2 tablespoons Corn Flakes, finely crushed

Thaw fillets, if frozen. Cut fish into serving portions and refrigerate. Cook onions and garlic in a skillet in butter or margarine until onions are soft but not browned. Add sauerkraut, wine, water, and caraway seeds. Cover and simmer for 30 minutes to blend flavors. While sauerkraut mixture is cooking, sprinkle fish with salt and roll in flour. Then arrange fish in a single layer in hot fat in a skillet and fry over moderate heat 4 to 5 minutes, or until fish is lightly browned. Add sour cream to sauerkraut mixture and turn into a baking dish about 8 by 12 inches in size.

Arrange fish in a single layer on sauerkraut. Mix cheese and corn flake crumbs and sprinkle over fish. Cover with aluminum foil, crimping it to the edges of the baking dish and bake in a moderate oven, 350°F., for 15 minutes. Remove aluminum foil cover and bake an additional 5 to 10 minutes, or until fish flakes easily when tested with a fork.

PERCH AND CHEESE SOUFFLE

6 servings

2 cups Perch, flaked
3 tablespoons Butter or Margarine
3 tablespoons Flour
½ teaspoon Salt
Dash Pepper

¼ teaspoon Worcestershire Sauce
2 to 3 drops Tabasco Sauce
¾ cup Milk
4 Eggs, separated
½ cup grated Cheese

Melt butter, blend in flour and add seasonings. Then add milk gradually and cook, stirring constantly, until mixture is thick and smooth. Stir a little of the hot sauce into the egg yolks and add this mixture to remaining sauce, stirring constantly. Blend in cheese and perch flakes. Fold in beaten egg whites. Then pour souffle mixture into a well-greased casserole dish. Place casserole dish in a pan of water and bake in a moderate oven, at 350°F., for 40 to 45 minutes, or until souffle is cooked in the center. Serve immediately.

FISH FLAKE POTATO PUFFS

6 servings

2 cups flaked Fish fillets	Dash Pepper
1 cup mashed Potatoes	3 Eggs, separated
1 tablespoon Butter or Margarine	1 tablespoon chopped Onion
⅓ cup Milk, scalded	2 tablespoons chopped Parsley
¾ teaspoon Salt	

Combine potatoes, butter, milk, seasonings, and egg yolks. Beat until light. Add onions, parsley, and fish flakes. Fold in stiffly beaten egg whites. Pour mixture into 6 well-greased individual casseroles. Place casserole dishes in a pan of water and bake in a moderate oven, at 350°F., for 30 to 35 minutes, or until fish-potato puffs are browned. Garnish and serve hot.

CATFISH CAPER

6 servings

2 pounds Catfish fillets, skinned	2 teaspoons Worcestershire Sauce
½ cup melted Fat or Cooking Oil	2 teaspoons Sugar
⅓ cup Lemon Juice	4 Bay Leaves, crushed
¼ cup chopped Onion	2 Garlic Cloves, finely chopped
2 tablespoons Capers and juice	¼ teaspoon Pepper
2 tablespoons Catsup	As desired Paprika
1 tablespoon Salt	

Thaw fillets, if frozen. Place in a single layer in a shallow baking dish. Combine all remaining ingredients except the paprika into a sauce and pour the sauce over the fillets. Let stand for 30 minutes, turning once. Remove fillets, reserving sauce for basting. Place fillets in well-greased baking dish and bake in a moderate oven, 350°F., for about 30 minutes, basting with remaining sauce occasionally. When fish flakes easily with a fork, sprinkle with paprika and serve.

FISH BAKED IN WINE SAUCE

6 servings

2 pounds Fish fillets
1 teaspoon Salt
Dash Pepper
½ cup Green Oinons and tops,
    thinly sliced

1 Lemon, thinly sliced
½ cup Catsup
2 tablespoons melted Fat or
    Cooking Oil
½ cup Dry White Wine

Thaw fillets, if frozen. Cut into serving size portions and place in a well-greased baking dish about 8 by 12 inches in size. Sprinkle fish with salt and pepper. Spread onion over fish and top with lemon slices. Combine catsup, oil, and wine into a sauce and pour over fillets. Bake in a moderate oven, 350°F., for 25 to 35 minutes, or until fish flakes easily when tested with a fork.

FISH FILLETS YUCATAN STYLE

6 servings

2 pounds Fish fillets
2 tablespoons Lemon Juice
1 teaspoon Salt
1 cup sliced Onions
¼ cup melted Fat or Oil

1 tablespoon Flour
½ cup sliced Stuffed Green Olives
¼ cup diced Pimientos
⅛ teaspoon Saffron (optional)
¾ cup Orange Juice

Thaw fish fillets, if frozen. Place fillets in a single layer in a well-greased baking dish, about 8 by 12 inches in size. Sprinkle lemon juice and salt over fish. Cook onions in a skillet in fat or oil until soft but not brown. Blend in flour. Add olives, pimientos, saffron, and orange juice. Cook, stirring constantly, until sauce is thickened. Then pour sauce over the fish. Bake in a moderate oven, at 350°F., for 20 to 25 minutes, or until the fish flakes easily when tested with a fork.

FISH WITH RAREBIT SAUCE

6 servings

2 pounds Fish fillets
1 tablespoon Lemon Juice
1½ teaspoons Salt
½ cup sliced Onions
2 tablespoons Butter or Margarine
2 tablespoons Flour

½ teaspoon Dry Mustard
½ teaspoon Paprika
1 cup Milk
½ cup Shredded Cheddar cheese
6 Tomato slices

Thaw fish, if frozen. Cut fillets into equal serving portions and place fish in a single layer in a well-greased baking dish, about 8 by 12 inches in area. Sprinkle with lemon juice and 1 teaspoon salt. Cook onions in a small saucepan in butter or margarine until tender but not brown. Blend in flour, mustard, paprika, and remaining ½ teaspoon salt. Add milk; cook, stirring constantly, until thickened.

Remove from heat; add cheese and stir until melted. Pour sauce over fish. Bake in a moderate oven at 350°F., for 20 to 25 minutes, or until fish flakes easily when tested with a fork. Garnish each serving with a tomato slice.

POLLOCK WITH CORN CHIPS

6 servings

2 pounds Pollock fillets
½ cup chopped Onions
3 tablespoons Butter or Margarine
2 tablespoons Flour
1 teaspoon Salt
1 (10-ounce) can frozen condensed
  Shrimp Soup

½ cup Half-and-Half milk & cream
1 (4-ounce) can sliced Mushrooms,
  undrained
1 (10-ounce) package frozen Peas,
  cooked and drained
3 cups Corn Chips

Thaw fish, if frozen. Cut fish into 1 inch chunks. Cook onions in butter or margarine in skillet until tender but not browned. Add fish and cook, turning carefully until it is firm. Sprinkle with flour and salt. Add soup, half-and-half, and undrained mushrooms. Heat and stir carefully. Fold in peas. Spread 2 of the cups of corn chips in even layers over the bottom of a baking dish about 8 by 12 inches in area. Add fish mixture. Sprinkle remaining one cup of corn chips around edge of fish. Bake in a moderate oven, about 350°F., for 25 to 30 minutes, or until mixture bubbles around the edges.

SALMON PIE

6 servings

2 pounds Salmon, fillets or steaks
1 teaspoon Salt
Dash Pepper
2 tablespoons Onion, grated
¼ cup Butter or other fat
¼ cup Flour

1 teaspoon Salt
Dash Pepper
2 cups Milk
1 quart Biscuit mix
1 cup cooked Peas
1 cup cooked Shrimp, cleaned

Cut fish into 1 inch chunks and sprinkle with salt, pepper, and grated onion. Melt butter and blend in flour, salt, and pepper. Add milk and cook until thick and smooth, stirring constantly. Prepare biscuit mix according to manufacturer's instructions and roll into layer about ⅛ of an inch thick. Line individual casserole dishes with the rolled biscuit mix. Place equal serving portions of fish in casseroles.

Combine the butter, milk, and flour sauce with peas and shrimp and pour over the fish in the casseroles. Cover each casserole with a top crust of biscuit mix. Bake in a hot oven, at 450°F., for 20 minutes, or until pies are brown.

FISH TAMALES

6 servings

2 pounds Fish steaks or fillets
1 cup Yellow Corn Meal
3 cups Water
4 teaspoons Salt
½ cup Green Pepper, chopped
½ cup Onion, chopped

5 tablespoons Butter or Margarine, melted
1 (No. 2½) can (or 3 cups) Tomatoes
2 teaspoons Chili Powder
2 tablespoons Flour
18 ripe Olives, pitted and sliced

Cut fish into bite-size cubes. Cook corn meal, water, and about 1¼ teaspoons of the salt in a pan over boiling water for approximately 30 minutes. Pour into a loaf pan and allow to set. Cook green pepper and onion in 3 tablespoons of the butter for about 5 minutes. Add tomatoes and remaining salt, and chili powder. Simmer 20 minutes. Add fish chunks to the tomato mixture and simmer 10 minutes longer.

Make a paste of the flour and remaining 2 tablespoons of butter; stir into the mixture. Add ripe olive slices. Line a well-greased casserole with a ¼ inch layer of corn meal mixture. Pour in salmon mixture and cover with remaining slices of corn meal. Bake in a moderate oven, about 375°F., for 40 minutes, or until brown.

PERCH TURBANS

6 servings

2 pounds Perch fillets
1 teaspoon Salt
Dash Pepper

1 quart Bread Stuffing*
¼ cup Butter or Margarine
3 slices Bacon

Skin fillets and sprinkle both sides with salt and pepper. Cut into slices to fit cups of a muffin tin. Grease muffin tin cups and line with the fillets so that ends of fillets overlap slightly. Place a ball of bread stuffing in the center of each circle of fish fillets. Brush tops with butter and place equal portions of bacon slices on each ball of stuffing. Bake in a moderate oven, 350°F., for 25 to 30 minutes, or until fish flakes easily with a fork. Serve on a heated platter, plain or with a sauce.
*Bread Stuffing (see p. 139)

BAKED FISH LOAF

6 servings

1 quart Fish flakes
3 cups Soft Bread Crumbs
1½ tablespoons chopped Parsley
2 tablespoons chopped Onion
1 teaspoon Salt
Dash Cayenne

½ teaspoon Celery Salt
¾ cup Milk
2 Eggs, beaten
1 tablespoon Lemon Juice
3 tablespoons Butter or Margarine, melted

Combine all ingredients and mix well. Place in a well-greased loaf pan. Bake in a moderate oven, about 350°F., for 40 to 45 minutes, or until loaf is firm in the center. Unmold on a heated platter. Garnish and serve.

FISH STEAKS HAWAIIAN

6 servings

2 pounds Fish steaks
1 teaspoon Salt
1 cup cooked Rice
1 cup Soft Bread Cubes
2 tablespoons Lemon Juice
1 cup crushed Pineapple, drained

½ teaspoon Curry Powder
¾ teaspoon Salt
2 tablespoons Butter or Margarine,
   melted
3 slices Bacon (optional)

Sprinkle fish steaks with salt. Combine rice, bread cubes, lemon juice, pineapple, curry powder, and salt in a mixture. Place one steak in a well-greased baking dish, about 8 by 10 inches in size. Place all or part of rice mixture on the steak and a second steak on top of the rice mixture. (Repeat if several small steaks rather than two large steaks are used.) Fasten steaks with rice mixture sandwiched between with small skewers or toothpicks. Brush top with butter and lay bacon slices on top. Bake in a moderate oven, 350°F., or until fish flakes easily when tested with a fork.

BAKED HALIBUT LOAF

6 servings

2 cups flaked Halibut
1 Chicken Bouillon Cube
¾ cup boiling Water
1½ cups Soft Bread Cubes
½ cup chopped Celery
1 tablespoon chopped Parsley

½ cup Cream, or half-and-half
1 teaspoon grated Onion
1 teaspoon Salt
Dash Pepper
2 teaspoons Lemon Juice
2 Eggs, beaten

Dissolve bouillon cube in boiling water. Combine all ingredients. Place in a well-greased loaf pan, about 6 by 9 inches in area. Bake in a moderate oven, 350°F., for 60 minutes, or until loaf is firm in the center.

HALIBUT WITH SHERRY

6 servings

2 cups Flaked Halibut
⅓ cup Butter or Margarine
3 tablespoons Flour
½ teaspoon Salt
2 cups Milk
1 tablespoon grated Onion
½ teaspoon Celery salt
½ teaspoon grated Lemon rind
1 tablespoon chopped Parsley

1 tablespoon chopped Green Pepper
¼ cup chopped Pimiento
3 drops Tabasco
1 Egg, beaten
½ cup Sherry
2 tablespoons Butter or Margarine, melted
½ cup dry Bread Crumbs

Melt ⅓ cup butter or margarine and blend in flour and salt. Add milk gradually and cook mixture until thick and smooth, stirring constantly. Add onion, celery salt, lemon rind, parsley, green pepper, and pimiento. Stir a little of the tabasco into the egg, then add to remaining sauce, stirring constantly. Add fish flakes and sherry and pour mixture into individual casserole dishes. Combine butter and bread crumbs and sprinkle over top of each casserole. Bake in a hot oven, at 400°F, for 10 to 15 minutes, or until brown.

STEELHEAD PIQUANTE

6 servings

1½ pounds Steelhead fillets
1 teaspoon Salt
1 medium Onion, sliced
1 Lemon, sliced

1 teaspoon mixed Pickling Spice
1 Garlic Clove, sliced
½ cup Mayonnaise
1 Cucumber, sliced

Salt steelhead on both sides. Arrange onion, lemon, spices and garlic on bottom of a well-greased casserole dish. Place the fish, skin side up, over the seasonings. Cover casserole and bake in a moderate oven, 350°F., for 60 minutes. Chill fish in casserole in refrigerator. After fish is chilled, place on a serving platter. Then remove the skin carefully. Garnish with mayonnaise and cucumber slices.

TANGY FISH BAKE

6 servings

2 pounds Fish fillets
¼ cup melted Butter or Margarine
1½ teaspoons Salt
1 cup chopped Onions
⅓ cup Catsup

⅓ cup Water
1 tablespoon Vinegar
1½ teaspoons prepared Mustard
1 teaspoon Worcestershire Sauce

Thaw fish fillets, if frozen. Cut fillets into equal serving portions. Place fish in a single layer, skin side down, in a well-greased baking dish, about 8 by 12 inches in size. Drizzle 2 tablespoons melted butter or margarine over fillets and sprinkle with ½ teaspoon salt. Cook onions in a skillet in remaining butter or margarine until tender but not brown. Add remaining ingredients, including 1 teaspoon of salt, to onions. Stir until hot and bubbly. Pour sauce over fish and bake in a moderate oven, at 350°F., 20 to 25 minutes, or until the fish flakes easily when fork tested.

ORANGE-PECAN FISH BAKE

6 servings

2 pounds Fish fillets
1 cup sliced Celery
⅓ cup chopped Onions
6 tablespoons Butter or Margarine
4 cups Soft Bread Cubes

½ cup chopped Pecans
1¼ teaspoons Salt
1 teaspoon grated Orange Rind
¼ cup Orange Juice

Thaw fish fillets, if frozen. Cut fillets into serving portions. Cook celery and onions in a skillet in ¼ cup of butter or margarine until tender but not brown. Stir in bread cubes, pecans, ¼ teaspoon salt, orange rind, and orange juice. Turn mixture into well-greased baking dish, about 8 by 12 inches in size. Arrange fish fillets in a single layer on the stuffing mixture. Melt remaining 2 tablespoons of butter or margarine and drizzle over the fish. Sprinkle with 1 teaspoon of salt. Bake in a moderate oven, at 350°F., for 25 to 30 minutes, or until fish flakes easily when tested with a fork. Serve with Cranberry-Orange Sauce (see p. 136)

PERCH AU GRATIN

6 servings

2 cups flaked Perch
¼ cup chopped Green Pepper
2 tablespoons Butter or Margarine, melted
2 tablespoons Flour
½ teaspoon Salt
Dash Pepper

1 cup Milk
½ cup grated Cheese
2 tablespoons Lemon Juice
2 tablespoons Butter or Margarine, melted
½ cup Dry Bread Crumbs

Cook green pepper in butter until tender. Blend in flour and seasonings. Add milk gradually and cook until thick, stirring constantly. Add cheese, lemon juice, and fish. Place in a well-greased casserole dish. Combine butter and bread crumbs and sprinkle over casserole. Bake in a hot oven, at 400°F., for 15 minutes, or until brown. Garnish and serve hot.

OLIVE-CAPER FISH BAKE

6 servings

2 pounds Fish Steaks
1 teaspoon Salt
¼ cup Butter or Margarine, melted
1 teaspoon Oregano

¼ teaspoon Pepper
¼ cup sliced, pitted ripe Olives
2 tablespoons Capers, drained
1 tablespoon Lemon Juice

Thaw fish, if frozen. Place steaks in a single layer in a well-greased baking dish, about 8 by 12 inches in size. Sprinkle with salt. Combine butter or margarine, oregano, and pepper. Mix well. Pour sauce over fish. Bake in a moderate oven, 350°F., for 20 to 25 minutes, or until fish flakes easily when fork tested. Place fish on a heated serving platter and keep warm. Reserve pan juices. Add olives, capers, and lemon juice to pan juices; heat and pour over fish.

NEW ENGLAND COD LOAF

6 to 8 servings

2 pounds Cod fillets
2 cups boiling Water
1 Onion, sliced
6 tablespoons Lemon Juice
2 teaspoons Salt
1½ cups Soft Bread Cubes
1 cup Milk

3 Eggs, beaten
1 cup sliced Celery
½ cup chopped Onions
2 tablespoons Butter or Margarine
2 tablespoons chopped Pimiento
1 teaspoon Worcestershire Sauce
2 cups Cranberry Sauce

Thaw fish, if frozen. Place fillets in a skillet. Add water and onion slices, ¼ cup of lemon juice and 1 teaspoon of salt. Cover and simmer for 5 to 10 minutes, or until fish flakes easily when tested with a fork. Remove fish from liquid. Drain and chill in a refrigerator. Then flake fish. Combine bread cubes, milk, and eggs and mix. Cook celery and chopped onions in butter or margarine in a small frying pan until tender. Combine pimiento, Worcestershire sauce, remaining two tablespoons of lemon juice, and 1 teaspoon salt and add to bread mixture, cooked fish, and vegetables. Mix well.

Press mixture of bread, fish, and vegetables evenly into a greased loaf pan, about 6 by 9 inches in size. Bake in a moderate oven, 350°F., for about 70 minutes, or until mixture is set. Let the cooked loaf stand about 10 minutes before turning out on a serving platter. Slice and serve with cranberry sauce. Cranberry Sauce (see p. 136)

OUTER BANKS MACKEREL

6 servings

3 to 4 pounds dressed Spanish
  Mackerel, or other dressed fish
1½ teaspoons Salt
¼ teaspoon Pepper

3 to 4 cups Vegetable Stuffing
2 tablespoons Butter or Margarine,
  melted

Thaw fish, if frozen. Clean, wash, and dry fish. Sprinkle inside and out with salt and pepper. Place fish on a well-greased bake-and-serve platter, about 12 by 18 inches in size. Stuff fish and brush with butter or margarine. Bake in a moderate oven, 350°F., for 30 to 45 minutes, or until fish flakes easily when tested with a fork.

HADDOCK AND VEGETABLES

6 servings

2 pounds Haddock fillets
1½ cups sliced Onions
1 Garlic Clove, minced
¼ cup Cooking Oil
2 cups Zucchini, sliced thinly
2 tablespoons Flour
1½ teaspoons Salt
¼ teaspoon Pepper

1 (16-ounce) can Tomatoes, or sliced
  fresh Tomatoes
1 (8-ounce) can Tomato sauce
1 teaspoon Basil
4 ounces, dry weight Spaghetti,
  cooked and drained
½ cup Parmesan Cheese, shredded

Thaw fish if frozen and cut fillets into 1 inch chunks. Cook onions and garlic in 2 tablespoons of cooking oil in a skillet; cook until tender but not browned. Add fish and cook, turning carefully, until fish is firm. Remove fish from pan. Add remaining cooking oil to pan, add zucchini and cook until thoroughly heated. Sprinkle with flour, salt, and pepper and mix. Add tomatoes, tomato sauce, and basil. Cook until sauce is thick and zucchini is almost tender, stirring occasionally. Combine with fish and mix carefully.

Layer half of the spaghetti, fish mixture, and cheese into a baking dish, about 9 by 12 inches. Repeat layers to use remaining ingredients and cover dish with aluminum foil, crimping it tightly to the edges of the dish. Bake in a moderate oven, at 350°F., for 20 minutes. Remove aluminum foil and continue baking another 20 minutes or until fish flakes easily when fork tested and zucchini is tender.

CITRUS SNAPPER

6 servings

2 pounds Snapper fillets
¼ cup grated Onion
2 tablespoons Orange Juice
2 tablespoons Lemon Juice

2 teaspoons grated Orange Rind
½ teaspoon Salt
⅛ teaspoon Nutmeg
⅛ teaspoon Pepper

Thaw fillets, if frozen. Cut fish into serving portions and place in a single layer, skin side down, in a well-greased baking dish, about 8 by 12 inches in size. Combine onion, orange and lemon juice, orange rind, and salt. Pour over fish. Cover and chill fish in marinade in a refrigerator for 30 minutes. Remove from refrigerator and sprinkle with nutmeg and pepper. Bake in a moderate oven, 350°F., for 25 to 30 minutes, or until fish flakes easily when tested with a fork.

97

FISH AND NOODLE CASSEROLE

6 to 8 servings

2 pounds Fish fillets
3 tablespoons Butter or Margarine
1 (3 to 4 ounce) can French Fried Onions
4 ounces, dry weight cooked Noodles, drained
1 (4-ounce) can sliced Mushrooms, drained
¼ cup chopped Pimientos
2 (10-ounce) cans Cheddar Cheese Soup
1 cup Milk
1 teaspoon Salt
1 teaspoon Paprika
1 teaspoon Worcestershire Sauce

Thaw fish, if frozen. Cut into 1 inch chunks. Cook fish in butter or margarine in a skillet, turning fish carefully, until firm. Combine fish, noodles, mushrooms, pimientos, and half of French fried onions in a large mixing bowl. Combine cheese soup, milk, and seasonings in a saucepan. Heat and stir until mixture is smooth. Pour over fish mixture and stir carefully. Pour combined mixture into a baking dish, about 9 by 12 inches in size. Bake in a moderate oven, 350°F., for 30 minutes, or until mixture is hot and bubbling around the edges. About 5 minutes before the end of baking time, sprinkle the remaining half of the onions around the edges.

BAKED BLACK DRUM

6 servings

2 pounds Black Drum fillets
½ cup Catsup
¼ cup Salad Oil
¼ cup Lemon Juice
1 tablespoon grated Onion
1 teaspoon Worcestershire Sauce
1 teaspoon Prepared Mustard
½ teaspoon Garlic Salt
¼ teaspoon Salt

Thaw fish, if frozen. Combine other ingredients in a shallow bowl. Add fillets, turning to moisten both sides with the sauce. Cover and place in a refrigerator to chill and marinate for 60 minutes. Remove fish from marinade and reserve sauce. Place fillets in a single layer in a well-greased baking dish, about 10 by 14 inches in size. Cover with remaining sauce and bake in a moderate oven, at 350°F., for 25 to 30 minutes, or until fish flakes easily when fork tested.

MICROWAVE
COOKING OF FISH

Microwave Cooking Tips:

1. Not only can fillets and steaks be cooked by microwaves, but whole fish, in spite of the irregular shape of the catch. As in conventional cooking, the thinner parts of the fish may be overcooked in comparison with the thcker parts; but if well-timed, the major portion will be tender and juicy. To cook a whole fish, wrap it in a large sheet of wax paper with the folded seam at the top. This makes it easier to check on the doneness of the fish. And don't forget that when any cover is removed from a cooking dish, hold it away from you so that any escaping steam will not burn you. The whole packaged fish can be placed on a microwave-proof trivet or on a couple of saucers turned upside down in a baking dish.

2. Little or no water is required on microwave cooking. A covered fish can be poached in its own juices and even cooked without the use of fats or oils. This is ideal for dieters, but if the flavor of a sauce, butter, or wine is desired, those flavors can be added with very little changes in the cooking time of the fish.

3. Fish sauces can be cooked in the microwave oven. Some of the sauces listed in a later chapter have microwave cooking directions.

4. Unless your microwave oven has the proper equipment for it, some processes may be done more easily on a conventional kitchen range. A quick turn under a broiler, for example, can give the fish a nice brown if your microwave oven is not equipped for browning.

5. Many of the preparations used for fish cookery, however, can be done with a microwave oven. Sauces can be mixed, cooked, and served in the same dish. Butter can be melted. Bacon for a crumbled topping can be cooked quickly. Crumbs can be dried and tossed with butter and herbs. Sprinkle these over the fish and heat during the last minute of cooking. Nut meats, which make a delicious topping on fish, can be blanched and toasted.

6. Herbs give a stronger flavor in microwave cookery. So be conservative in the use of herbs in any fish recipes or the herb flavor may be overpowering.

7. To get more juice from lemons used in fish recipes, heat one in the microwave oven for about 15 seconds.

8. Because microwave cooking is moist cooking, fresh bread has a tendency to get soggy when heated with other, moister foods. Therefore, it is better to start with a dry bun or a slightly dry slice of bread; it will freshen up to your satisfaction during cooking.

MICROWAVE FISH SANDWICH

1 piece of cooked Fish fillet,
sandwich size
1 Bun
  or 2 slices of Bread, slightly dry

As desired Mayonnaise or other
  spread
As desired Cheese (optional)

Place the piece of cooked fish fillet on a bun or bread slice, with mayonnaise or other desired spread. Heat on a paper plate or wrapped in a paper napkin for about 45 seconds. 3 or 4 sandwiches will take several minutes to heat. If a fish-and-cheese sandwich is desired, pop the cheese slice into the sandwich after removing it from the oven. The cheese will melt during the standing time. Let sandwiches stand about 1 minute before eating; otherwise, they can burn your mouth.

FISH STEAKS CURACAO

4 to 6 servings

2 pounds Fish steaks, about ¾
inch thick
2 tablespoons Butter
½ teaspoon grated Orange Rind

3 tablespoons Plain Yogurt
1 tablespoon Curacao
As desired Salt
As desired Pepper

Thaw fish, if frozen. Pat dry on paper toweling. In the microwave oven, melt butter with grated orange rind in a non-metal baking dish about 8 by 10 inches in size, for 30 seconds. Stir in yogurt and Curacao. Place fish in a single layer in dish with sauce and cook for 3½ minutes uncovered. Turn fish over, cover dish, and cook 2 to 3 minutes more. Check to see if fish is opaque and flesh flakes easily when fork tested. Season with salt and pepper to taste.

SNAPPERS WITH SHRIMP SAUCE

4 to 5 servings

1½ pounds Red Snapper or other
   fish fillets
1 (6 ounce) can cleaned Shrimp
2 tablespoons Butter
½ cup Milk
½ cup Heavy Cream
1 tablespoon Brandy

2 tablespoons Flour
¼ teaspoon Salt
¼ teaspoon White Pepper, freshly
   ground
Dash Cayenne
As needed Paprika (for garnish)

In a blender, puree shrimp with juice. Set aside. In a large heat resistant measuring cup melt butter about 30 seconds. Blend in milk, heavy cream, brandy, flour, salt, pepper, and cayenne. Cook until thickened, stirring at 1-minute intervals, for about 4 minutes. Blend in pureed shrimp, stirring well. Place fillets in ovenproof baking dish. Cover and cook in microwave oven 3 minutes. Turn fish over and cover with sauce. Sprinkle on paprika. Cook, uncovered for 2 to 3 minutes. Let stand 1 to 2 minutes, then check to see if fish flakes easily when fork tested.

FILLET OF PIKE AU GRATIN

4 to 6 servings

2½ to 3 pounds Pike fillets
2 tablespoons Butter
2 tablespoons Flour
1 cup Chicken Stock
1 tablespoon Onion, finely chopped
1 tablespoon Lemon Juice

1 tablespoon Minced parsley
¼ teaspoon Salt
¼ teaspoon Pepper
As desired Bread Crumbs, toasted
   for garnish

Melt the butter in a large measuring cup for 30 seconds. Blend in the flour, and add the chicken stock, onion, lemon juice, parsley, salt and pepper. Cook for 2 minutes, stirring at 1 minute. Arrange fillets in baking dish and pour sauce over them. Cover and cook for 3 minutes. Turn fish. Scoop up some of the sauce and pour it over the top of the fish. Cook an additional 3 minutes, remove from oven and let stand 3 minutes. Sprinkle on toasted bread crumbs. Place under broiler of conventional stove for light browning, if desired.

BLACK BASS WITH WALNUTS

4 to 6 servings

2½ to 3 pounds Whole Black Bass,
scaled and cleaned
½ teaspoon Salt
1 tablespoon Butter
¾ cup Walnut Meats, chopped

1 cup Sour Cream
⅓ cup Lemon Juice
½ teaspoon Horseradish, grated
¼ teaspoon Salt

Remove head, tail, fins, and the skin surrounding them. Sprinkle ½ teaspoon salt inside fish. Wrap in large sheet of wax paper, with folded seam at top. Place on microwave-proof trivet in a baking dish. Cook for 3 minutes. Rotate the dish half a turn. Cook another 3 minutes. Do not remove covering. Then let stand for 3 minutes.

In an ovenproof casserole heat butter for 15 seconds. Add walnut meats, and cook for 3 minutes, stirring at 1 minute intervals. Combine the sour cream, lemon juice, horseradish, and salt with any liquid that has formed from the cooked fish (but no more than ½ cup). Combine this mixture with the walnuts in the casserole and heat 30 seconds. Serve with the bass.

FAST AND FANCY FISH

6 servings

2 pounds Fish fillets
¼ cup Garlic French Dressing
1 tablespoon Soy Sauce

¼ teaspoon Ground Ginger
As needed Lime slices, for garnish

Thaw fish, if frozen. Place in a single layer in a baking dish. Combine French dressing, soy sauce, and ginger. Pour sauce over fillets and marinate 10 minutes. Cook, uncovered for 2 minutes. Turn fish, cover, and cook an additional 2 or 3 minutes. Let stand, covered, for 2 minutes. Check for doneness. Serve with slices of fresh lime.

SHRIMP STUFFED TROUT SESAME

2 servings

2 (8 ounces each) Rainbow Trout, pan-dressed
1 (6-ounce) can cleaned Shrimp, drained, chopped
½ cup Celery, chopped
1 tablespoon Onion, chopped
⅛ teaspoon Pepper
2 tablespoons Toasted Sesame Seeds
1 tablespoon Butter

Combine shrimp, celery, onion and pepper. Arrange trout in baking dish and stuff with shrimp dressing. Top with sesame seeds and dot with butter. Cover and cook 2 minutes in microwave oven. Give dish one-half turn. Cover and cook 2 minutes longer. Then let stand for 2 to 3 minutes. Check for doneness.

BREAKFAST KIPPERED HERRING

4 servings

4 (8-ounces each) Kippered Herrings
2 tablespoons Butter
Dash Tabasco Sauce
1 tablespoon Worcestershire Sauce
2 tablespoons Lemon Juice

Arrange kippers in a baking dish that is microwave-proof. In a measuring cup, combine butter, Tabasco sauce, Worcestershire sauce, and lemon juice. Heat about 30 seconds until butter has melted. Stir and pour over herring. Cover and cook 2 minutes. Give dish one-half turn. Cook 2 minutes more. Let stand 2 to 3 minutes. If fish is done, it should flake easily when tested with a fork. Serve with scrambled eggs.

STURGEON MADEIRA

2 to 3 servings

1 pound Sturgeon Steaks	1 tablespoon Butter
3 tablespoons Madeira Wine	1 teaspoon Capers, minced
2 tablespoons Dill Pickle, chopped	1 teaspoon Olives, minced
1 tablespoon fresh Parsley, chopped	

Thaw fish, if frozen. Cut steaks into equal serving portions. Arrange fish steaks in microwave-proof baking dish. Season with Madeira, half the dill pickle, and the parsley. Dot with butter. Cover and cook 2 minutes. Sprinkle steaks with the rest of the pickle, the capers and the minced olives. Cover and cook an additional 2 minutes. Let stand for 1 to 2 minutes. Check to see if fish flakes easily when fork tested.

SPRING BASS WITH DANDELION GREENS

3 servings

1 pound Bass fillets	1 cup Sour Cream
1 pound Dandelion Greens	As needed Paprika, for garnish
2 teaspoons Lemon Juice	

Wash dandelion greens, drain. With only water that clings to leaves, cook, covered in a microwave-proof baking dish for 3 minutes. Arrange fish on dandelion greens. Sprinkle lemon juice on fish. Cook, covered, for 2 minutes. Spread sour cream on fillets. Give dish one-half turn. Cook 2 minutes more, covered. Garnish with paprika and let stand 2 to 3 minutes. Fish is ready to serve if it flakes easily when tested with a fork.

FISH FILLETS WITH SPICED ONIONS

6 servings

2 pounds Fish fillets   As desired Salt
2 tablespoons Butter   As desired Pepper
3 tablespoons Spiced Onion Sauce   Spiced Onion Sauce*
1 teaspoon chopped Parsley

Thaw fillets, if frozen, and pat dry. In a shallow baking dish melt butter for 30 seconds in microwave oven. Place fillets in a single layer (making sure the butter coats bottom of dish evenly) and cook, with dish covered, for 2 minutes. Turn the fish over and top with spiced onion sauce, parsley, and salt and pepper. Cover and cook for 3 minutes more. Let stand, covered for 2 minutes. Check to see if fish is done. Serve with fresh parsley.
*Spiced Onion Sauce (see p. 134)

LAKE SALMON SAUTERNE

2 to 3 servings

1 pound Lake Salmon fillets   2 teaspoons Shallots, chopped
2 tablespoons Dry Sauterne Wine   1 cup Parsley Sauce

Prepare sauce and let stand. Arrange fish in microwave-proof baking dish. Season with wine and chopped shallots. Cover and cook until fish is opaque and flakes easily when fork tested, or about 3 minutes. Serve with Parsley Sauce. Parsley Sauce recipe (see p. 136)

SLOW-COOKER
COOKING OF FISH

Slow-Cooking Tips:

1. Always thaw fish before cooking.
2. Use smaller amounts of liquid because there is little evaporation in crock cooking. Use about half the amount required for conventional cooking of fish.
3. Dieters can take advantage of slow-cooking since moist cooking allows fish to be prepared without fats. Fillets or small whole pan fish can be steamed to perfection in 30 minutes on the *HIGH* setting of a slow-cooker.
4. When making fish chowder or soup in a slow-cooker, cook the vegetables first and add the fish during the last 30 minutes.
5. Use the slow-cooker to keep a sauce such as Hollandaise sauce warm and ready for the fish. It will hold well for hours.
6. Fish stocks can be made and clarified in the slow-cooker, ready for soups and aspics.

FISH STOCK

1½ pounds Fish heads, tails, bones, skin, and trimmings
½ cup Onion, chopped
½ cup Parsley, minced
1 medium Carrot, chopped
½ cup Celery, chopped
3 to 4 Peppercorns
3 to 4 Cloves
1 Bay leaf
½ teaspoon Thyme
½ teaspoon Lemon Rind, grated
2 teaspoons Lemon Juice
½ cup White Wine
2 cups Water

In slow-cooker, combine fish trimmings with rest of ingredients. Cover and cook on *LOW* 4 hours. Strain the stock and use for soups, sauces, and aspics.

For conventional stovetop cooking:

In a kettle or large saucepan, add the ingredients listed above for Fish Stock, and bring mixture to a boil. Reduce heat to a moderate cooking temperature and simmer 20 to 30 minutes. Strain stock. Fish stock may be refrigerated for several days or frozen for a period of several weeks.

To Clarify Stock for Aspic

1 quart cool Fish Stock
2 Egg Shells, crushed
2 Egg Whites, lightly beaten

Combine the liquid with egg shells and egg whites in a slow-cooker. Set heat on *LOW* and cook until a foam appears, about 20 to 30 minutes. Turn off slow-cooker and let stock stand about 10 minutes. Line a sieve with a double layer of cheesecloth. Gently push the foam to one side and ladle the stock through the sieve into a container. Cool and store, covered, in a refrigerator.

For conventional stovetop cooking:

Combine the liquid, egg shells, and egg whites in a large saucepan or kettle. Bring the mixture to a simmer very slowly. Do not allow it to boil. If stock boils when clarifying, it must be redone. Simmer stock 15 to 20 minutes. Remove pot from heat carefully and let stand about 10 minutes. Strain stock as directed.

DIET WHITING

1 serving

1 (6 to 8-ounce) Whiting, cleaned, head removed

½ Lemon, thinly sliced
2 cups Water, boiling

Put water in a slow-cooker. Place whiting on a steamer rack that fits in a slow-cooker, making sure the water does not come over the rack. Place lemon slices over fish. Cover and cook on *HIGH* setting for 30 minutes, or until fish flakes easily when fork tested.

Author's note: Whiting is an ideal source of protein for persons on weight reducing diets. A pound of whiting flesh contains only 476 calories, or slightly less than 30 calories per ounce. And there are no carbohydrates to worry about.

COD WITH NEW POTATOES

4 servings

4 New Potatoes, medium size
1 pound Cod fillets

¼ cup Butter or Margarine
1 tablespoon Dill, chopped

Wash potatoes in skins. Drain but do not dry. Place in slow-cooker, cover and cook on *LOW* setting for 6 hours. Lay fillets, cut into serving size pieces, on top of potatoes. Dot with butter and sprinkle on dill. Cook on *LOW* setting for 1 hour, or on *HIGH* for 30 minutes. Fish should flake easily when fork tested at end of cooking time.

POACHED PIKE

6 servings

2 to 3 pounds Pike
1 cup Dry White Wine
½ Bay Leaf
1 Shallot, or Green Onion, chopped

1 Parsley sprig
¼ teaspoon Thyme
½ teaspoon Salt
Dash Pepper

Wrap the fish in cheesecloth and place in a slow-cooker. Pour in wine. Add rest of ingredients. Cover pot and cook on *LOW* setting for 2 to 3 hours, or on *HIGH* setting for 1 to 2 hours. When pike flakes easily remove from slow-cooker. Strain poaching liquid into a container, cover, and refrigerate, or use immediately in preparing a sauce. (See Sauces, p. 129) The pike can be served hot with a sauce, cold with salad greens, or prepared as an aspic. *(See Special Recipes,* (p. 119)

FISH PUDDING

6 servings

1½ pounds Fish fillets
4 Egg Yolks
2 Bread slices
1½ cups Milk
¼ pound Butter

1 teaspoon Salt
½ teaspoon Pepper
½ teaspoon Nutmeg
4 Egg Whites

Remove any skin or bones from fish and flake fish. Add egg yolks one at a time, stirring each in well. Remove crusts from bread and soak bread in milk. Add milk and bread mixture to fish and egg mixture. Stir in butter, salt, pepper, and nutmeg. Stiffly beat egg whites and fold into mixture. Pour into a greased mold (about 2 quarts in size) and cover with several napkins. Put a small amount of water in the bottom of a slow cooker and add the fish mold. Cook on *LOW* setting for 3 hours.

SOUPS, CHOWDERS AND STEWS

Think chowder and you probably are thinking of a fish chowder, perhaps in a large, steaming kettle. In fact, the word chowder gets its name from the old iron cauldron once used to cook soups and stews in a kitchen fireplace. Fish soups can be the quickest and easiest of the various kinds of chowders, stews, and soups, because they cook so readily.

Chowder Tips:
1. To preserve the delicate texture of fish when making soups or chowders, remove the pot from the heat almost before the fish reaches the flaking stage and serve the soup quickly and hot.
2. Simmer a fish chowder or soup, but never boil it.
3. Use home-made fish stock as part or all of the liquid in the soup for heightened flavor.
4. Clam broth can be substituted for a basic fish stock.
5. Dry white wine is delicious in fish soups, but remember to go easy on the salting as wine tends to bring out a salty flavor. Add wine not too long before serving and then correct the seasoning.
6. Add herbs during the last half hour of cooking a fish soup or chowder. Their flavor, too, is intensified by longer cooking which can drown out the light flavor of a fish.
7. For a different and savory addition to fish chowder, add a few fresh marigold petals.
8. A quick fish chowder can be made from a vegetable soup by adding a cup of diced fish fillets and simmering for 5 minutes.

FISH CHOWDER
---

6 servings

1 pound Fish steaks or fillets	2 cups Milk
2 tablespoons Bacon, diced	1 teaspoon Salt
¼ cup Onions, chopped	Dash Pepper
2 cups hot Water	As desired chopped Parsley
1 cup Potatoes, diced	

Cut fish into half-inch cubes. Fry bacon until crisp. Add onion, and cook until slightly browned. Add water and potatoes; cook 10 minutes or until potatoes are partially tender. Add fish and simmer for 10 minutes longer, or until fish flakes easily when fork tested. Add milk and seasonings; heat. Serve immediately with chopped parsley sprinkled over the top.

FISH AND ONION SOUP

6 servings

1 pound Fish fillets or steaks	2 tablespoons Flour
4 Chicken Bouillon Cubes	½ teaspoon Salt
1 quart boiling Water	Dash Pepper
1 quart sliced Onion	Dash Paprika
¼ cup Butter or other Fat, melted	½ cup grated Cheese

Remove skin and bones from fish steaks or fillets; cut into 1 inch cubes. Dissolve bouillon cubes in boiling water. Cook onion in butter until tender. Blend in flour and seasonings. Add bouillon gradually and heat until boiling, stirring constantly. Add fish and simmer for 10 minutes. Garnish with cheese sprinkled over the top.

BOUILLABAISSE

6 servings

1 pound Fish fillets	1 cup Water
½ cup chopped Onion	1¼ teaspoons Salt
½ cup chopped Celery	¼ teaspoon Thyme
¼ cup Butter or Margarine, melted	1 Bay Leaf, crushed
1 Garlic Clove, finely chopped	Dash Pepper
1 (7-ounce) can Clams, minced	As desired Grated Parmesan Cheese
1 (5-ounce) can Shrimp, drained	6 slices French Toast
1 (20-ounce) can Tomatoes	

Remove skin and any bones from fillets; cut into ½ inch cubes. Cook onion, celery, and garlic in butter until tender. Add remaining ingredients except cheese and bread. Bring to boiling point and simmer for 20 minutes. Sprinkle cheese over bread; toast. Arrange toast in large soup bowls and cover with the bouillabaisse.

FLOUNDER SOUP GOURMET

6 servings

2 pounds Flounder fillets
1 Onion, sliced
3 Parsley sprigs
1 slice Lemon
1 Bay Leaf
4 Allspice, whole
4 Peppercorns
1 Garlic Clove, finely chopped

1 quart Water
¼ cup Butter or Margarine
¼ cup Flour
2 teaspoons Salt
3½ cups Fish Stock and Water
1 cup Coffee Cream
¼ cup chopped Parsley

Remove any skin and bones from fish and cut into ¼ inch cubes. Place trimmings in saucepan with water, onion, parsley, lemon, bay leaf, allspice, peppercorns, and garlic; cover and simmer for 30 minutes. Strain and save fish stock. Melt butter; blend in flour and salt. Add fish stock gradually and cook until thick and smooth, stirring constantly. Add fish; simmer for 10 minutes. Add cream; heat. Garnish with parsley.

PERCH TOMATO SOUP

6 servings

1 pound Perch fillets
¼ cup diced Bacon
½ cup chopped Onion
½ cup chopped Celery
2 cups boiling Water

1½ teaspoons Salt
Dash Pepper
⅓ cup uncooked Rice
2 cups Tomato Juice
As desired chopped Parsley

Skin fillets and cut into 1 inch pieces. Fry bacon until crisp and brown. Add onion and celery; cook until tender and slightly brown. Add water, seasonings, and rice; cook 10 minutes. Add fish, cook 10 minutes longer or until fish and rice are tender. Add tomato juice; heat. Serve immediately with chopped parsley over the top.

CATFISH GUMBO

6 servings

1 pound skinned Catfish fillets
½ cup chopped Celery
½ cup chopped Green Pepper
½ cup chopped Onion
1 Garlic Clove, finely chopped
¼ cup melted Butter or Cooking Oil
2 Beef Bouillon Cubes
2 cups boiling Water

1 (16-ounce) can Tomatoes
1 (10-ounce) package Frozen Okra
2 teaspoons Salt
¼ teaspoon Pepper
¼ teaspoon Thyme
1 Bay Leaf
Dash Liquid Hot Pepper
1½ cups hot cooked Rice

Thaw fillets if frozen. Cut into 1-inch pieces. Cook celery, green pepper, onion, and garlic in butter or oil until tender. Dissolve bouillon cubes in water. Add bouillon, tomatoes, okra, and seasonings. Cover and simmer for 30 minutes. Add fish. Cover and simmer for 15 minutes longer or until fish flakes easily when tested with a fork. Remove bay leaf. Place ¼ cup rice in each of 6 soup bowls. Fill with gumbo.

ALASKAN FISHERMAN'S STEW

6 servings

2 pounds Rockfish fillets
1½ cups sliced Celery
½ cup chopped Onion
1 Garlic Clove, minced
¼ cup Butter or Margarine
1 (28-ounce) can Tomatoes, undrained
1 (8-ounce) can Tomato Sauce
2 teaspoons Salt

½ teaspoon Paprika
¼ teaspoon Chili Powder
¼ teaspoon Pepper
1 (7-ounce) package Spaghetti, uncooked
2 cups boiling Water
¼ cup Grated Parmesan Cheese

Thaw fish if frozen and cut into 1 inch chunks. Cook celery, onion, and garlic in butter or margarine in large, heavy pan until tender. Add tomatoes, tomato sauce, and seasonings. Bring to a simmer. Cover and cook slowly for 15 to 20 minutes. Add uncooked spaghetti and boiling water. Mix and cover pan. Cook slowly about 10 minutes or until spaghetti is almost tender. Add fish, cover and cook slowly for another 10 minutes, or until fish flakes easily when fork tested. Serve hot with cheese sprinkled over the top.

BASS STEW WITH CORNBREAD DUMPLINGS

6 to 8 servings

2 pounds Bass fillets
1½ cups sliced Onions
¼ cup Butter or Margarine
1 (10-ounce) package Frozen Mixed
   Vegetables, partially defrosted
1 (4-ounce) can sliced Mushrooms,
   undrained
2 (10½-ounce) cans Condensed Cream
   of Celery Soup

1 cup Milk
1 teaspoon Salt
¼ teaspoon Leaf Thyme
4 slices Bacon, diced
9 to 10 ounces Commercial Corn
   Muffin Mix
As desired Milk

Thaw fish if frozen. Cut fish into 1 inch pieces. Cook onions in butter or margarine until tender but not browned in a 6 quart Dutch oven with heat-proof handles, stirring often. Add frozen vegetables and mix. Add mushrooms, soup, milk, salt, and thyme. Heat and stir until hot. Fold in fish. Cover and bake in a hot oven, at about 400 degrees F., for 15 minutes or until hot and bubbly.

Fry bacon until crisp; drain on paper towels. Prepare muffin mix according to manufacturer's directions but reducing milk by half. Stir in crisp bacon lightly and drop 6 to 8 mounds of batter onto the hot fish mixture. Return to oven and bake for 20 minutes or until dumplings are done and fish flakes easily.

NORTHWEST CIOPPINO

6 to 8 servings

1½ pounds Sea Bass
2 cups sliced Onion
2 Garlic Cloves, finely minced
¼ cup Olive Oil or other
   cooking oil
1 (28-ounce) can Italian Tomatoes,
   undrained
1 (8-ounce) can Tomato Sauce

1 cup Water
¼ cup chopped Parsley
2 teaspoons Salt
1 teaspoon Basil
½ teaspoon Oregano
¼ teaspoon Pepper
12 Clams, in shell, washed
1 cup Shrimp, cooked, peeled

Thaw fish if frozen and cut into 1 to 2-inch chunks. Cook onion and garlic in oil until onion is tender but not brown. Add tomatoes, tomato sauce, water, parsley, salt, basil, oregano, and pepper. Cover. Simmer gently for about 30 minutes. Add fish chunks; cover and simmer 10 to 20 minutes. Add clams in shells and shrimp; cover and cook 10 minutes longer or until fish flakes easily when tested with a fork.

CREOLE-STYLE BOUILLABAISSE

8 servings

1 pound Red Drum or other
  fish fillets
1 pound Sea Trout or other
  fish fillets
½ pound raw, peeled, deveined
  Shrimp
1 pint Oysters
1 (6-½ ounce) can Crabmeat, drained,
  cartilage removed
2 tablespoons Butter or Margarine
2 tablespoons Olive Oil
¼ cup all-purpose Flour
1 cup chopped Onion

½ cup chopped Celery
1 Garlic Clove, minced
5 cups Water
1 (16-ounce) can Tomatoes,
  undrained, cut up
½ cup Dry White Wine
2 tablespoons chopped Parsley
1 tablespoon Lemon Juice
1 Bay Leaf
½ teaspoon Salt
¼ teaspoon Saffron
¼ teaspoon Cayenne Pepper

Thaw fish and shellfish if frozen. Remove skin and bones from fish and cut each fish into equal serving portions. Melt margarine or butter in a 5 or 6 quart Dutch oven. Add olive oil and blend in flour. Cook, stirring constantly, until light brown in color. Add onion, celery, and garlic. Cook, stirring constantly, until vegetables begin to brown. Gradually stir in water. Add tomatoes, wine, parsley, lemon juice, bay leaf, salt, saffron, cayenne pepper, and about one-fourth of the pieces of fish. Bring to a boil and simmer for 20 minutes. Add remaining fish and cook 5 to 8 minutes longer. Add shrimp, oysters and crabmeat, and cook another 4 or 5 minutes or until all the seafood is properly cooked.

SALMON CREAM SOUP

6 servings

1½ pounds Salmon steaks or fillets
2 cups hot Water
1 slice Onion
1 stalk Celery
1 sprig Parsley
1 (1-inch) piece Green Pepper

1 quart Milk
5 tablespoons Butter or Margarine
5 tablespoons Flour
2½ teaspoons Salt
Dash Pepper
As desired chopped Parsley

Remove skin and bones from fish and grind twice. Stir into hot water and simmer gently for 3 minutes, stirring constantly. Add onion, celery, parsley, and green pepper to milk. Scald and strain. Melt butter; blend in flour, salt, and pepper. Add scalded milk, and cook until thick and smooth, stirring constantly. Add to fish mixture. Heat and serve immediately with parsley garnish.

117

HEARTY POLLOCK CHOWDER

6 to 8 servings

2 pounds Pollock fillets
2 cups sliced Carrots
2 cups raw Potatoes, diced
2 cups sliced Onions
2 teaspoons Salt
1 teaspoon Dill Weed
2 whole Cloves

1 small Bay Leaf
¼ cup Butter or Margarine
2 cups boiling Water
½ cup Dry White Wine
1 cup Half-and-Half (milk/cream)
2 tablespoons Flour
2 tablespoons chopped Parsley

Thaw fish if frozen. Cut fillets into 1 to 2 inch pieces. Refrigerate. Combine carrots, potatoes, onions, salt, dill weed, cloves, bay leaf, and butter or margarine in a 6 quart Dutch oven. Add boiling water. Cover and bake in a moderate oven, 375 degrees F., for 40 minutes, or until vegetables are tender. Add fish and wine; cover and cook for an additional 20 minutes or until fish flakes easily when fork tested. Combine half-and-half with flour; blend until smooth and add to chowder. Stir carefully until hot and slightly thickened. Sprinkle with parsley and serve hot.

ASPICS, CREPES
AND OTHER
SPECIAL RECIPES

There are many different, interesting, and tasty ways of preparing fish in addition to the methods previously described. This chapter includes recipes that have been used since colonial days in America. Plantation Fish in Aspic is an example of a recipe popular in the Carolinas when that area was still a British colony.

PLANTATION FISH IN ASPIC

6 servings

2 pounds Grouper or other fish fillets
3 cups Court Bouillon
½ cup cold Water
2 envelopes Unflavored Gelatin
¼ cup Tarragon Vinegar
2 tablespoons Lemon Juice
1 teaspoon Dry Mustard

¼ cup chopped Celery
¼ cup chopped Green Onion
¼ cup chopped Green Pepper
2 tablespoons chopped Pimiento
2 tablespoons chopped Parsley
As desired Salad Greens
As desired Mayonnaise

Court Bouillon

2 cups Boiling water
1 cup Sauterne wine
1 medium Onion, quartered
1 Celery Stalk, quartered
2 Bay Leaves

1½ teaspoons Salt
¼ teaspoon dried Thyme Leaves, crushed
1 Lemon

Add all ingredients except lemon to boiling water and mix carefully. Cut lemon in half, squeeze in juice, then drop halves into court bouillon. Place fish fillets in a well-greased skillet. Add court bouillon. Cover and simmer for 5 to 10 minutes or until fish flakes easily when tested with a fork. Remove fish and set aside to cool. Strain court bouillon and save.

In a 4 cup measure, place ½ cup cold water and stir in unflavored gelatin to soften. Add court bouillon and stir to dissolve gelatin. Add vinegar, lemon juice, and enough water to make 4 cups of liquid. Stir in remaining liquid. Chill to consistency of unbeaten egg whites. Remove skin and bones from fish and flake fish into small pieces.

Mix together fish, celery, green onion, green pepper, pimiento, and parsley. Fold together fish mixture and gelatin and turn into a lightly oiled loaf pan, or a 7-cup mold. Chill until firm. Unmold on a serving dish lined with salad greens. Serve with mayonnaise.

GULF COURT BOUILLON

6 servings

2 pounds Red Drum or other
   fish fillets
⅓ cup Margarine or Butter
½ cup all-purpose Flour
1½ cups chopped Onion
1 cup chopped Celery
½ cup chopped Green Onion
½ cup chopped Green Pepper
2 tablespoons chopped Parsley
1 Garlic Clove, minced
2 (15-ounce) cans Tomato Sauce
   with Tomato Bits

¾ cup Dry Red Wine
2 tablespoons Lemon Juice
½ teaspoon Salt
½ teaspoon dried Thyme Leaves,
   crushed
¼ teaspoon dried Marjoram Leaves,
   crushed
¼ teaspoon Cayenne Pepper
6 Allspice, whole
1 Bay Leaf
As needed Lemon slices

Remove skin and bones from fish and cut into equal serving portions. In a 4 or 5-quart Dutch oven, heat oil, blend in flour. Cook, stirring constantly, over medium heat until light brown in color, about 10 minutes. Add onion, celery, green onion, green pepper, parsley, and garlic. Cover and cook five minutes or until tender. Gradually stir in tomato sauce. Add wine, lemon juice, thyme, marjoram, cayenne, allspice, and bay leaf. Bring to a boil and simmer for 30 minutes. Add fish to court bouillon. Cover and simmer five to 10 minutes or until fish flakes easily when fork tested. To serve, place portion of fish in a soup bowl and pour about one cup of sauce over the fish. Garnish with lemon slices.

HALIBUT DIABLE

6 servings

2 cups flaked Halibut or other fish
2 tablespoons Coffee Cream
6 slices Buttered Toast
1 cup Mayonnaise or other salad
   dressing
⅓ cup Chili Sauce

2 teaspoons prepared Mustard
2 drops Tabasco
½ teaspoon Vinegar
½ teaspoon Paprika
½ teaspoon Celery Salt

Combine fish and cream; mix well. Arrange toast on a baking sheet and cover each slice with fish mixture. Combine remaining ingredients. Cover fish with mayonnaise mixture. Bake in a moderate oven, 350 degrees F., for 15 minutes, or until brown.

6 servings

2 pounds Pompano or other fish fillets

¼ pound Shrimp, cooked, peeled, deveined

3 cups Water

1 teaspoon Salt

2 slices Lemon

1 Bay Leaf

⅛ teaspoon Dried Thyme Leaves, crushed

6 sheets Parchment or brown paper

2 tablespoons Cooking Oil

½ cup chopped Green Onion

1 Garlic Clove, minced

2 tablespoons Butter or Margarine

3 tablespoons all-purpose Flour

¼ teaspoon Salt

2 Egg Yolks, slightly beaten

3 tablespoons Dry White Wine

1 (7-ounce) can Crabmeat, drained, flaked, and cartilage removed

Thaw fish, if frozen. Chop shrimp. Put water, one teaspoon of salt, lemon, bay leaf, and thyme in a skillet and bring to a boil. Add fish, cover and simmer for about 10 minutes, or until fish flakes easily when tested with a fork. Carefully remove fish.

Reserve and strain stock, saving one and one-half cups. Remove skin and bones from fish. Cut parchment or brown paper into six heart-shaped pieces, measuring about 10 by 12 inches each. Brush paper with oil. Place one fillet on half of each paper heart. In a saucepan melt butter or margarine, add onion and garlic, and cook until tender. Blend in flour and ¼ teaspoon of salt. Add reserved stock. Cook, stirring constantly, until thickened. Gradually stir small amount of mixture into egg yolks; add to remaining sauce, stirring constantly. Heat until mixture begins to thicken. Stir in wine, crabmeat, and shrimp. Heat.

Spoon about ½ cup of sauce over each fillet. Fold over other half of paper heart to form individual cases around fillet. Seal cases, starting at top of heart, by turning edges up and folding, twisting tip of heart to hold cases closed. Place paper cases in shallow baking pan and bake in a hot oven, 400 degrees F., for 10 to 15 minutes. To serve, cut cases open with large X-shaped design on top; fold back each segment.

POLLOCK AND SPAGHETTI

6 servings

2 pounds Pollock or other fish fillets
2 cups sliced Onions
2 Garlic Cloves, minced
¼ cup Cooking Oil
1 (28-ounce) can Tomatoes
1 (8-ounce) can Tomato Sauce
1 (4-ounce) can sliced Mushrooms,
   drained

1½ teaspoons Salt
1½ teaspoons Basil
1 teaspoon crushed Rosemary
6 servings hot cooked Spaghetti
As desired Parmesan Cheese,
   shredded

    Thaw fish, if frozen, and cut into 1 inch chunks. Cook onions and garlic in oil in a 6-quart Dutch oven until tender. Add tomatoes, tomato sauce, mushrooms, ½ teaspoon salt, and herbs. Cover and simmer for 20 minutes, or until flavors are blended. Uncover and simmer another 10 minutes, until sauce is thickened. Add fish and remaining 1 teaspoon of salt. Simmer uncovered for an additional 10 minutes, or until fish flakes easily when fork tested. Spoon fish mixture over spaghetti and sprinkle generously with Parmesan cheese.

SMOKY SABLEFISH SALAD

6 servings

1 cup Mayonnaise, or other salad
   dressing
1 teaspoon prepared Mustard
½ teaspoon Tarragon leaves
½ teaspoon Salt
¼ teaspoon Celery Seed
3 cups cooked Potatoes, sliced,
   chilled

2 cups Celery, sliced
⅔ cup Radishes, sliced
⅓ cup Green Onions, sliced
½ pound Smoked Sablefish,
   flaked
As needed Lettuce Leaves

    Combine salad dressing, mustard, tarragon, salt, and celery seed, and mix well. Fold in sliced potatoes. Cover; refrigerate for several hours to blend flavors. Add celery, radishes, onion, and flaked fish; mix carefully. Arrange on lettuce-lined serving dish with additional sablefish, or tuna, or shrimp as garnish.

BASS SLAW

6 servings

1½ pounds Bass fillets
1 quart boiling Water
1 tablespoon Salt
¼ cup Mayonnaise or other salad
  dressing
2 tablespoons chopped Onion
2 tablespoons Sweet Pickle Relish

1 tablespoon Lemon Juice
1 teaspoon Salt
1 cup shredded Green Cabbage
1 cup shredded Red Cabbage
6 Lettuce cups
As needed Lemon Wedges

Thaw fillets if frozen. Place fillets in boiling salted water. Cover and simmer about 10 minutes or until fish flakes easily when tested. Drain. Remove skin and bones and flake fish. Combine salad dressing, onion, relish, lemon juice, salt, and fish. Chill at least 1 hour to blend flavors. Add cabbage and toss lightly. Serve in lettuce cups with lemon wedges.

FISH FOO YUNG SESAME

6 servings

1 pound Smoked Whitefish or other
  smoked fish
1 (16-ounce) can Bean Sprouts, drained
6 Eggs, beaten
½ cup Green Onion, finely chopped

Dash Pepper
1¾ cups Foo Yung Sauce
1 tablespoon Sesame Seeds

Remove skin and bones from fish and flake fish. Combine all ingredients except Foo Yung sauce and sesame seeds. Pour ⅓ cup fish mixture onto a hot greased griddle or skillet and fry at moderate heat for 2 or 3 minutes, or until brown. Turn carefully and fry 2 or 3 minutes longer. Drain on absorbent paper towels. Pour Foo Yung sauce over patties and sprinkle with sesame seeds.

Foo Yung Sauce:

2 Chicken Bouillon Cubes
½ teaspoon Sugar
2 cups boiling Water

2 tablespoons Cornstarch
2 tablespoons Soy sauce

Dissolve bouillon cubes and sugar in boiling water. Combine cornstarch and soy sauce. Add cornstarch mixture to bouillon mixture and cook until thick and clear, stirring constantly. Serve with fish.

MOLDED PERCH SALAD

6 servings

2 cups Flaked Perch
1 tablespoon Gelatin
¼ cup cold Water
½ cup boiling Water
½ cup Mayonnaise or other salad
  dressing
¼ cup Catsup
2 tablespoons Lemon Juice

½ cup chopped Celery
2 tablespoons chopped Sweet
  Pickle
2 tablespoons chopped Stuffed
  Olives
¼ teaspoon Salt
As desired Salad Greens

Soften gelatin in cold water for 5 minutes, then add boiling water and stir until dissolved. Cool. Blend mayonnaise, catsup, and lemon juice. Combine all ingredients except salad greens; mix well. Pour into mold and chill until firm. Unmold on salad greens and garnish.

FLOUNDER AVOCADO COCKTAIL

6 servings

2 cups Flaked Flounder or other fish
1 cup Cocktail Sauce
1 cup Avocado cubes

As desired Parsley
As desired Lemon Wedges

Cocktail Sauce:

¾ cup Catsup
¼ cup Lemon Juice
¼ teaspoon Salt

6 drops Tabasco
3 tablespoons Celery, finely
  chopped

Combine all cocktail sauce ingredients and chill. Arrange layers of cocktail sauce, avocado, and fish in cocktail glasses. Begin and end with cocktail sauce. Garnish with parsley and lemon wedges.

PICKEREL SANDWICH LOAF

6 servings

1 pound Pickerel or other fish fillets
1 cup boiling Water
1 slice Onion
2 tablespoons Lemon Juice
¾ teaspoon Salt
1 loaf unsliced Vienna Bread

½ cup Salad Dressing
½ cup Chili Sauce
½ cup chopped Dill Pickles
¼ cup sliced Green Onions
1 tablespoon Horseradish
1 cup Cheddar Cheese, shredded

Place fish in a skillet. Add water, onion, lemon juice, and half teaspoon of salt. Cover and simmer 5 to 10 minutes, or until fish flakes easily. Remove fish, drain, chill, and flake. Cut bread loaf in half, lengthwise; hollow out top and bottom halves and save bread pieces from inside loaf. Combine bread pieces with remaining ingredients and flaked fish. Fill bread shell with mixture, with top shell over filling. Wrap loaf in aluminum foil and bake in a hot oven, 400 degrees F., for 40 minutes. Cut in thick chunks or slices for serving.

SMOKED FISH DIP

Makes 1¾ cups

½ pound Smoked Whitefish or other
    smoked fish
1 cup Sour Cream
2 tablespoons Lemon Juice
2 tablespoons chopped Chives
1 teaspoon Minced Onion, instant
½ teaspoon Salt

¼ teaspoon Dried Rosemary
6 Peppercorns, crushed
Dash ground Cloves
As desired chopped Parsley,
    assorted Chips, Crackers, or
    Raw Vegetables

Remove skin and bones from fish and flake fish. Combine all ingredients except parsley and chips or crackers. Chill at least 1 hour to blend flavors. Sprinkle dip with parsley. Serve with chips, crackers, or raw vegetables.

6 servings

Crepes:

½ cup Milk

1 Egg

½ cup sifted Flour

¼ teaspoon Salt

Combine milk, egg, flour, and salt; heat until smooth. Fry crepes one at a time in lightly greased skillet, using 3 tablespoons of batter for each crepe. Pour batter into skillet, tilt pan quickly so that batter will cover bottom of pan. Cook until lightly browned on both sides, turning once. Stack and keep warm while preparing filling.

Filling:

1 cup White-fleshed fish fillets

½ cup thinly sliced Celery

2 tablespoons thinly sliced Green Onions

¼ cup Salad Dressing

2 tablespoons diced Pimiento

1 teaspoon Curry Powder

1 teaspoon Lemon Juice

½ teaspoon Worcestershire Sauce

Thaw fish if frozen and combine with celery, onion, salad dressing, pimiento, curry powder, lemon juice, and Worcestershire sauce; mix carefully. Spread an equal amount of filling over each crepe, and roll up. Arrange filled crepes on heat-proof platter. Cover with aluminum foil, crimping edges of foil around platter. Bake in a moderate oven at 350 degrees F., about 15 minutes, or until well heated. Prepare sauce while crepes are heating.

Sauce:

1 (10-ounce) can frozen, condensed Shrimp Soup

½ cup Milk

½ cup cooked small Shrimp

1 teaspoon Lemon Juice

Combine soup, milk, shrimp, and lemon juice; warm to serving temperature over low heat, stirring constantly. Pour sauce over crepes when ready to serve.

6 servings

1 pound Pollock or other fish fillets	¼ cup Butter or Margarine
1 cup boiling Water	1 (10-½ ounce) can Condensed
¼ cup Lemon Juice	Cream of Mushroom Soup
1 slice Onion	½ cup Sour Cream
½ teaspoon Salt	2 tablespoons diced Pimiento
¾ cup chopped Celery	12 Herbed Pancakes
¼ cup chopped Onions	

Herbed Pancakes:

3 Eggs	½ teaspoon Fines herbes blend
1½ cups Milk	1½ cups sifted Flour
¾ teaspoon Salt	¾ teaspoon Baking Powder

Combine eggs, milk, salt, and herbes; beat well. Sift flour and baking powder together; add to other ingredients; beat until smooth. For each pancake, pour one-fourth cup of batter into lightly buttered skillet. Tilt and rotate pan quickly so that batter covers bottom of pan. Brown on underside; turn and brown other side.

Thaw fish if frozen and place fish in a skillet. Add boiling water, 2 tablespoons of lemon juice, onion, and salt. Cover and simmer 5 to 10 minutes or until fish flakes easily when fork tested. Carefully remove fish from liquid, drain, and chill. Flake fish. Sauté celery and onions in 3 tablespoons of butter or margarine until tender. Add soup; stir well. Add sour cream, pimiento, and remaining lemon juice; stir. Reserve 1 cup of soup mixture for top. Fold flaked fish into remaining soup mixture. Spread an equal amount of fish mixture, about ¼ cup, over pancakes and roll up. Place in a baking dish, about 8 by 12 inches in dimensions.

Brush with remaining melted butter or margarine. Cover with aluminum foil, crimping tightly to edges of baking dish. Bake in a moderate oven, 375 degrees F., for 20 minutes, or until heated. Remove foil. Spoon reserved soup mixture over pancakes and return to oven for 5 minutes before serving.

SAUCES
AND STUFFINGS

SAUCES

The sauce recipes presented on the following pages are intended to be as simple as possible in preparation. There are more traditional and complex ways of preparing some fish sauces. However, these are designed to give you a variety of fish sauces that are simple, quick, and effective in enhancing the flavors of a wide range of fish species.

Sauce Tips:
1. Using an electric blender in sauce cookery, once viewed by chefs as almost heretical, is becoming an increasingly popular technique. Why not, if the alternative is to run out and buy a jar of prepared sauce? If you are not familiar with sauce making or would hesitate to use a wire whisk, try a blender sauce.
2. Use your own judgment about the choice of butter or margarine in making a sauce. People who do not use butter should not be condemned to sauceless meals.
3. Except for the basic structure of a recipe that makes it hang together — the egg yolks, the fats, flour, or amount of liquid — you can usually make substitutions or variations in a sauce recipe. If you prefer a bit more or less of a particular herb, go ahead and adjust the recipe to your own taste buds. Or if, say, you are on a low sodium diet, leave out the salt and let the guests add their own from a salt shaker.
4. Some suggestions for varying sauces are included. But feel free to create your own variations and enjoy your sauce making.

HOLLANDAISE SAUCE (Blender)

Makes 1 cup sauce

3 Egg Yolks   Dash Cayenne Pepper
2 tablespoons Lemon Juice   ½ cup Butter or Margarine

Mix egg yolks, lemon juice, and cayenne pepper in a blender. Turn blender on and off, quickly, while blender is covered. Heat butter, or margarine, until it is melted and almost boiling. Turn blender to High Speed and add melted butter slowly, blending until sauce is thick and all butter has been added; about 30 seconds. Pour sauce into a container and heat over warm, not hot, water until ready to serve. Hollandaise sauce may be refrigerated or frozen and rewarmed for later use.

Variations:

MOUSSELINE SAUCE
---

1 cup Hollandaise Sauce
½ cup Whipped Cream

Stir in whipped cream and mix carefully just before serving. Serve hot or cold with poached fish.

CUCUMBER HOLLANDAISE SAUCE
---

1 Cucumber, peeled, seeded
1 cup Hollandaise Sauce
1 teaspoon Chives, chopped

Chop cucumber and drain thoroughly by squeezing in cheesecloth. Add about ¼ to ½ cup to Hollandaise sauce. Stir in chives.

FIGARO SAUCE
---

1 cup Hollandaise Sauce   1 tablespoon Parsley, finely
1 tablespoon Tomato Paste   chopped
1 teaspoon Worcestershire Sauce

Combine ingredients and mix carefully.

BERNAISE SAUCE (Blender)

Makes 1 cup sauce

1 tablespoon Green Onion, chopped
2 teaspoons Lemon Juice
¼ cup Dry White Wine
½ teaspoon Dried Tarragon Leaves

¼ teaspoon Chervil Leaves
3 Egg Yolks
⅛ teaspoon Cayenne Pepper
½ cup Butter or Margarine

In saucepan combine green onion, lemon juice, white wine, tarragon, and chervil. Simmer until mixture is reduced to about 2 tablespoons. Cool. Pour herb mixture into blender and add egg yolks and cayenne. Cover and turn blender on and off, quickly. Heat butter or margarine until melted and almost boiling. Turn blender to High Speed and add butter in a slow, steady stream, blending until thick; about 30 seconds. Pour sauce into a container and heat over warm, not hot, water until ready to serve.

Variation:

CHORON SAUCE

1 cup Bernaise Sauce
¼ cup Tomato Paste or Puree

Combine ingredients, mix carefully, and serve with broiled fish.

MAYONNAISE (Blender)

Makes 1 cup

1 cup Salad Oil, or part Olive Oil
2 Eggs
2 tablespoons Lemon Juice
½ teaspoon Sugar

1 teaspoon Prepared Mustard
½ teaspoon Salt
¼ teaspoon White Pepper

In a blender put ¼ cup oil, eggs, lemon juice, sugar, mustard, salt, and pepper. Whirl on High Speed about 5 seconds. Turn off blender. Again blend on High Speed and add remaining oil in a slow, steady stream. Oil must be added very slowly to allow egg and oil to combine properly. If necessary, stop blender and clean sides with rubber spatula. Blend until thick and smooth. Pour into container and chill.

Variations:

GREEN MAYONNAISE
---

1 cup Mayonnaise
1 tablespoon Parsley, fresh, minced
1½ teaspoons Chives, minced

1½ teaspoons Tarragon, fresh,
  minced
½ teaspoon Dill, fresh, minced
½ teaspoon Chervil, fresh, minced

Combine ingredients, mix carefully. Chill.

TARTAR SAUCE
---

1 cup Mayonnaise
1 Sweet Pickle, finely chopped
1 tablespoon Onion, grated
1 tablespoon Parsley, fresh, minced

1 tablespoon Capers, minced
½ teaspoon Dried Tarragon
½ teaspoon Dried Chervil
1 teaspoon prepared Mustard

Combine ingredients, mix carefully. Chill.

HORSERADISH MAYONNAISE
---

1 cup Mayonnaise
2 tablespoons Horseradish, fresh, grated

Combine and mix carefully just before serving.

REMOULADE SAUCE (Blender)

Makes 1¼ cups sauce

¼ cup Tarragon Vinegar
2 tablespoons prepared Brown Mustard
1 tablespoon Catsup
1½ teaspoons Paprika
½ teaspoon Salt
¼ teaspoon Cayenne Pepper

½ cup Salad Oil
¼ cup Celery, chopped
¼ cup Green Onion, chopped
1 tablespoon Parsley, fresh,
  chopped

In a blender place vinegar, mustard, catsup, paprika, salt, and cayenne pepper. Add salad oil slowly to other ingredients while blender is whirling constantly. When ingredients are thoroughly mixed, pour into a container and stir in celery, green onion, and parsley. Refrigerate 3 to 4 hours to allow flavors to combine properly.

ORANGE AND GREEN GRAPE SAUCE

1 tablespoon Cornstarch
1 tablespoon Sugar
½ cup Orange Juice
½ cup cold Water
2 teaspoons grated Orange Rind

1 teaspoon Lemon Juice
1 (11-ounce) can Mandarin Orange
  Segments, drained
1 cup seeded Green
  Grape Halves

Combine cornstarch and sugar in a saucepan. Add orange juice and cold water. Stirring constantly, cook over low heat until sauce is thick. Stir in orange rind, lemon juice, and fruits. When thoroughly heated and mixed, serve with poached fish.

LOW-CALORIE FISH SAUCE

⅓ cup low-calorie
  French Dressing
2 tablespoons Lemon Juice

2 tablespoons Soy Sauce

Mix all ingredients. Cover and refrigerate until ready to serve. Use as a marinade or a dressing with hot or cold fish dishes.

SPICED ONION (INDIA) SAUCE (Blender)

1 medium Onion, peeled
1 medium Tomato, peeled
2 Garlic Cloves
⅛ teaspoon Powdered Ginger

1 teaspoon Curry Powder
¼ cup Tomato Juice
1 tablespoon White Vinegar

Chop onion and tomato into blender. Add garlic cloves, ginger, and curry powder. Blend, adding tomato juice and vinegar gradually. Whirl until smooth and creamy. Pour sauce into a jar with a tight lid; it will stay fresh, if stored in a refrigerator, for about 1 week. Serve with poached or steamed fish, in chowders, or any curry.

CLARIFIED OR DRAWN BUTTER

Drawn butter is preferred by many cooks in frying or sautéeing fish because it does not smoke or overly brown fish as whole butter tends to do. To prepare drawn or clarified butter for cooking fish or other foods, heat ¼ pound of butter in a saucepan over low heat without stirring. Cool. Then carefully pour off the liquid fat that has separated from the solids. Save in a container for use in cooking.

Microwave Oven Directions:

Put butter in a glass measuring cup or bowl. Heat in microwave oven two minutes 30 seconds, or until it is melted and bubbling. Remove from oven. When oil has separated from solids, pour off.

DRAWN BUTTER SAUCE

Makes 1 cup

2 tablespoons Drawn Butter
2 tablespoons Flour
½ teaspoon Salt

Dash Pepper
1 cup Hot Fish Stock

Melt butter and blend in flour with seasonings. Add fish stock and cook slowly, stirring constantly, until thickened.

Variations:

ANCHOVY SAUCE

1 cup Drawn Butter Sauce
½ teaspoon Anchovy Paste

Mix carefully.

CAPER SAUCE

1 cup drawn Butter Sauce
¼ cup Capers, drained

Combine and mix carefully over heat.

MINT SAUCE

1 cup drawn Butter Sauce
⅛ cup Mint Leaves, fresh, chopped

Mix carefully.

PARSLEY SAUCE

1 cup drawn Butter Sauce
1 tablespoon Lemon Juice

1 tablespoon Parsley, fresh,
chopped

Mix carefully.

CRANBERRY-ORANGE SAUCE

Makes 1¼ cups sauce

⅓ cup Sugar
2 teaspoons Cornstarch
½ cup Orange Juice

½ cup Water
1 cup raw Cranberries
2 teaspoons grated Orange Rind

Combine sugar and cornstarch in a 2 quart saucepan and mix. Add orange juice and water and cook, stirring constantly until mixture comes to a boil. Add cranberries and cook 5 minutes or until skins on cranberries pop, stirring occasionally. Fold in orange rind. Serve with hot or cold fish.

CRANBERRY SAUCE

Makes 1¾ cups sauce

1 tablespoon Sugar
1 tablespoon Cornstarch
1 (10-ounce) package frozen Cranberry
  with Orange, defrosted

¾ cup Water
1 tablespoon Lemon Juice
1 teaspoon grated Lemon Rind

Combine sugar and cornstarch; add cranberry with orange, water, and lemon juice. Cook, stirring constantly until thickened and clear. Stir in lemon rind. Serve with baked fish.

WHITE SAUCE

Makes 1 cup sauce

2 tablespoons Butter or Margarine   ⅛ teaspoon Pepper, black or white
2 tablespoons Flour   1 cup Milk
¼ teaspoon Salt

In a saucepan, melt butter or margarine over low heat. Blend in the flour and seasonings, stirring constantly, for about 3 to 4 minutes. Slowly add the milk, still stirring. Simmer the sauce, stirring, until it is thick and smooth.

Microwave Oven Directions: (Same ingredients as above)
In a 2 cup microwave-proof measuring cup melt butter, about 30 seconds. Blend in flour, salt, and pepper. Heat about 30 seconds. Stir in milk slowly until smooth. Cook 2 minutes 45 seconds, or until sauce reaches desired thickness. To prevent lumping, stir at one-minute intervals. Remove from oven and continue stirring until smooth.

Variations:
Instead of 1 cup of milk, substitute 1 cup of fish stock, or fish stock combined with milk, or fish stock with cream.

PARSLEY WHITE SAUCE

1 cup White Sauce
2 tablespoons Parsley, fresh, chopped

When white sauce is removed from heat, stir in chopped parsley.
Add a dash of grated nutmeg, or hot sauce, or Worcestershire sauce. Put in a teaspoon of lemon juice, or curry powder, or white wine. There are a number of herbs that go well with fish and can be blended into white sauce. But use the herbs with caution because they can dominate the flavor of the sauce. A half cup of sauteed mushrooms stirred into a white sauce makes a variation recommended for steamed fish dishes.

Author's note: Other ways of adding variety to the white sauce include — stir in 2 tablespoons of chopped chives, or grated Parmesan cheese. Or, add 1 tablespoon of chopped capers. Or pickles. Blend in freshly grated horseradish, or drained prepared horseradish.

SAUCE A LA KENNEDY

Makes 1 cup sauce

½ cup Mayonnaise
¼ cup prepared Steak Sauce
2 tablespoons Lemon Juice

1 tablespoon prepared Mustard
Dash Liquid Hot Pepper Sauce

Combine all the ingredients and mix carefully. Chill before using.

SOUR CREAM AND HORSERADISH SAUCE

Makes 1⅓ cups sauce

1 cup Sour Cream
3 tablespoons Horseradish, shredded,
    or prepared but drained
1 tablespoon Onion, finely chopped

1 tablespoon fresh Dill, finely
    chopped
¼ teaspoon Salt
⅛ teaspoon White Pepper

Combine ingredients, mix carefully. Chill. Serve with cold poached fish or smoked trout.

SOUR CREAM AND MUSTARD SAUCE

Makes 1⅓ cups sauce

1 Egg Yolk, beaten
1 teaspoon prepared Mustard
1 tablespoon Onion, finely chopped

2 tablespoons Wine Vinegar
1 cup Sour Cream
Dash Cayenne

Mix the beaten egg yolk with the mustard and onion. Blend in the vinegar. Combine the egg yolk mixture with the sour cream and add the dash of cayenne pepper. Serve cold.

MUSTARD SAUCE

1 cup White sauce
1 teaspoon prepared Mustard

When white sauce is removed from heat, stir in mustard. For a stronger flavor, stir in ½ teaspoon dry mustard when blending flour into melted butter.

SOUR CREAM AND CUCUMBER SAUCE

Makes 1½ cups sauce

1 cup Sour Cream
½ cup Cucumber, peeled,
  seeded, grated
2 tablespoons Chives, chopped

½ teaspoon Lime Peel,
  freshly grated
½ teaspoon Salt

Combine ingredients and chill. Serve with poached or smoked fish.

STUFFINGS

As the term suggests, a stuffing is a preparation of complementary foods stuffed into the body cavity of a fish just before it is placed in an oven for baking. However, stuffings, which usually consist of mixtures of light, bland, moist foods, such as bread, rice, vegetables, etc., also are used as a bed on which to place fish fillets for cooking. And stuffing materials also may be folded or rolled with fish fillets, as in turbans.

Stuffings should not include raw food items that require high cooking temperatures to render them edible because internal temperatures of stuffing in a fish seldom reach 170 degrees F. or higher during the relatively short cooking time required for the tender flesh of fish.

· A rule of thumb is to plan on 1 cup, or less, of stuffing per pound of fish. If the stuffing is placed in the body cavity of the fish, the opening should be closed with small skewers or wooden toothpicks; clean string can be laced across the wooden picks as added insurance that the stuffing will not spill out of the body cavity.

BREAD STUFFING

Makes about 5 cups

3 tablespoons Onion, chopped
¾ cups Celery, chopped
6 tablespoons Butter or other Fat,
  melted
1 teaspoon Salt

Dash Pepper
1 teaspoon Thyme (or sage, or
  savory seasoning)
4 cups Bread Crumbs, day-old or soft

Sauté onion and celery in butter or other fat for about 10 minutes or until tender. Combine with rest of ingredients. Mix thoroughly. If stuffing is too dry, add 1 tablespoon water, milk, fish stock, or lemon juice.

Variations:
  Add 2 to 3 tablespoons chopped parsley.
  Omit herbs, and add ½ cup nut meats.
  Or, omit herbs and add ½ cup piccalilli.

VEGETABLE STUFFING

Makes 3½ cups

½ cup Butter or Margarine
1½ cups Onion, chopped
1 cup Celery
1 cup Mushrooms, fresh, chopped
½ cup Green Pepper, chopped

1 Garlic Clove, minced
2 Tomatoes, peeled,
  seeded, and chopped
3 cups Bread Crumbs, soft
½ teaspoon Salt

In saucepan, melt butter or margarine. Add all ingredients except bread and seasoning. Cover and cook until tender. Combine with bread crumbs and salt. Mix thoroughly.

ORANGE-RICE STUFFING

Makes about 4 cups

1 cup Celery with leaves,
  chopped
¼ cup Onion, chopped
¼ cup Butter or Margarine,
  melted
¾ cup Water
¼ cup Orange Juice

2 tablespoons Lemon Juice
1 tablespoon Orange Rind, grated
¾ teaspoon Salt
1 cup pre-cooked Rice
½ cup Almonds, toasted,
  blanched, slivered

Sauté celery and onion in butter or margarine until tender. Add water, juices, grated orange rind, and salt. Bring to a boil. Add rice and stir to moisten. Cover and remove from heat. Let stand 5 minutes. Add almonds. Mix thoroughly.

CARROT STUFFING

Makes about 5 cups

4 cups Soft Bread Crumbs
1 cup grated Carrots
2 tablespoons Pimiento, chopped
1 tablespoon Onion, finely chopped

¼ teaspoon Salt
⅛ teaspoon Pepper
¼ cup Butter or Margarine,
  melted

Combine bread, carrots, pimiento, onion, salt, and pepper. Add ¼ cup melted butter or margarine. Stir until well mixed.

INDEX